SELECTED POEMS

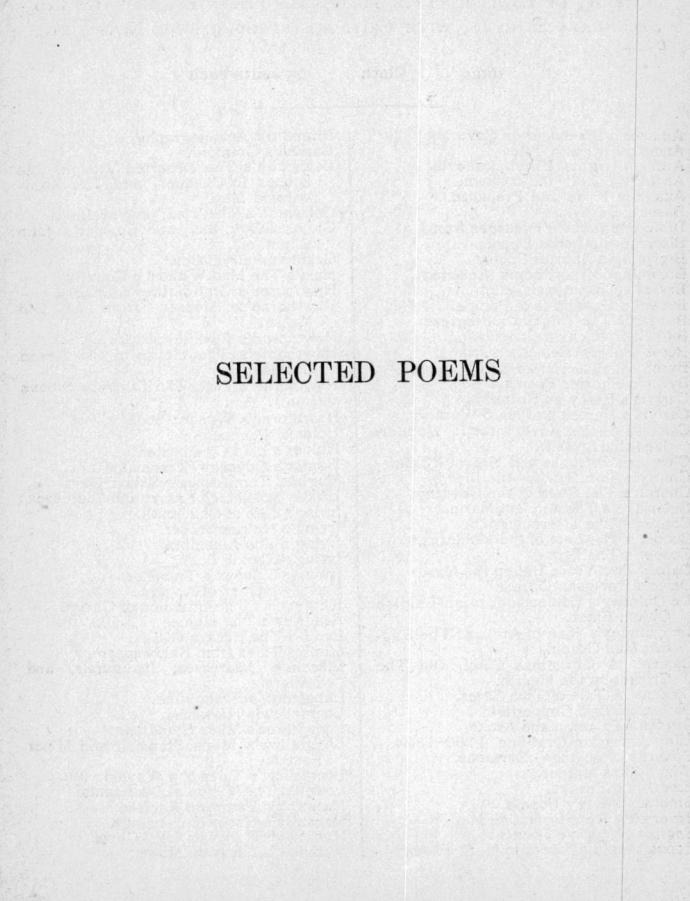

Macmillan's Pocket American and English Classics

A SERIES OF ENGLISH TEXTS, EDITED FOR USE IN ELEMENTARY AND SECONDARY SCHOOLS, WITH CRITICAL INTRODUCTIONS, NOTES, ETC.

16mo   Cloth   25 cents each

- **Addison's Sir Roger de Coverley.**
- **Andersen's Fairy Tales.**
- **Arabian Nights' Entertainments.**
- **Arnold's Sohrab and Rustum.**
- **Austen's Pride and Prejudice.**
- **Bacon's Essays.**
- **Bible (Memorable Passages from).**
- **Blackmore's Lorna Doone.**
- **Browning's Shorter Poems.**
- **Browning, Mrs., Poems (Selected).**
- **Bryant's Thanatopsis, etc.**
- **Bulwer's Last Days of Pompeii.**
- **Bunyan's The Pilgrim's Progress.**
- **Burke's Speech on Conciliation.**
- **Burns' Poems (Selections from).**
- **Byron's Childe Harold's Pilgrimage.**
- **Byron's Shorter Poems.**
- **Carlyle's Essay on Burns.**
- **Carlyle's Heroes and Hero Worship.**
- **Carroll's Alice's Adventures in Wonderland (Illustrated).**
- **Chaucer's Prologue and Knight's Tale.**
- **Church's The Story of the Iliad.**
- **Church's The Story of the Odyssey.**
- **Coleridge's The Ancient Mariner.**
- **Cooper's The Deerslayer.**
- **Cooper's The Last of the Mohicans.**
- **Cooper's The Spy.**
- **Dana's Two Years Before the Mast.**
- **Defoe's Robinson Crusoe.**
- **De Quincey's Confessions of an English Opium-Eater.**
- **De Quincey's Joan of Arc, and The English Mail-Coach.**
- **Dickens' A Christmas Carol, and The Cricket on the Hearth.**
- **Dickens' A Tale of Two Cities.**
- **Dickens' David Copperfield.**
- **Dryden's Palamon and Arcite.**
- **Early American Orations, 1760–1824.**
- **Edwards' (Jonathan) Sermons.**
- **Eliot's Silas Marner.**
- **Emerson's Essays.**
- **Emerson's Early Poems.**
- **Emerson's Representative Men.**
- **English Narrative Poems.**
- **Epoch-making Papers in U. S. History.**
- **Franklin's Autobiography.**
- **Gaskell's Cranford.**
- **Goldsmith's The Deserted Village, She Stoops to Conquer, and The Good-natured Man.**
- **Goldsmith's The Vicar of Wakefield.**
- **Gray's Elegy, etc., and Cowper's John Gilpin, etc.**
- **Grimm's Fairy Tales.**
- **Hale's The Man Without a Country.**
- **Hawthorne's Grandfather's Chair.**
- **Hawthorne's Mosses from an Old Manse.**
- **Hawthorne's Tanglewood Tales.**
- **Hawthorne's The House of the Seven Gables.**
- **Hawthorne's Twice-told Tales (Selections from).**
- **Hawthorne's Wonder-Book.**
- **Holmes' Poems.**
- **Homer's Iliad (Translated).**
- **Homer's Odyssey (Translated).**
- **Hughes' Tom Brown's School Days.**
- **Huxley's Selected Essays and Addresses.**
- **Irving's Life of Goldsmith.**
- **Irving's Knickerbocker.**
- **Irving's The Alhambra.**
- **Irving's Sketch Book.**
- **Irving's Tales of a Traveller.**
- **Keary's Heroes of Asgard.**
- **Kempis, à: The Imitation of Christ.**
- **Kingsley's The Heroes.**
- **Lamb's The Essays of Elia.**
- **Lamb's Tales from Shakespeare.**
- **Lincoln's Addresses, Inaugurals, and Letters.**
- **Longfellow's Evangeline.**
- **Longfellow's Hiawatha.**
- **Longfellow's Miles Standish.**
- **Longfellow's Miles Standish and Minor Poems.**
- **Longfellow's Tales of a Wayside Inn.**
- **Lowell's The Vision of Sir Launfal.**
- **Macaulay's Essay on Addison.**
- **Macaulay's Essay on Hastings.**
- **Macaulay's Essay on Lord Clive.**
- **Macaulay's Essay on Milton.**

CONTENTS

	PAGE
INTRODUCTION	
The Poems	ix
Coleridge and Wordsworth	xi
Macaulay and the Lays	xiv
Poe and The Raven	xix
Lowell and The Vision of Sir Launfal	xxiii
Arnold and Sohrab and Rustum	xxvi
Longfellow and The Courtship of Miles Standish	xxix
Whittier and Snow-Bound	xxxi
THE RIME OF THE ANCIENT MARINER	1
LAYS OF ANCIENT ROME	
Horatius	33
The Battle of the Lake Regillus	64
Virginia	101
The Prophecy of Capys	123
THE RAVEN	138
THE VISION OF SIR LAUNFAL	147
SOHRAB AND RUSTUM	164
THE COURTSHIP OF MILES STANDISH	202
SNOW-BOUND	237
NOTES	321

vii

SELECTED POEMS

FOR REQUIRED READING IN SECONDARY SCHOOLS

EDITED

WITH INTRODUCTION AND NOTES

BY

HENRY W. BOYNTON, M.A.

New York
THE MACMILLAN COMPANY
1915

All rights reserved

COPYRIGHT, 1911,

BY THE MACMILLAN COMPANY.

Set up and electrotyped. Published November, 1911. Reprinted
July, 1912; September, 1912; February, 1915.

Norwood Press
J. S. Cushing Co. — Berwick & Smith Co.
Norwood, Mass., U.S.A.

Macmillan's Pocket American and English Classics

A SERIES OF ENGLISH TEXTS, EDITED FOR USE IN ELEMENTARY AND SECONDARY SCHOOLS, WITH CRITICAL INTRODUCTIONS, NOTES, ETC.

16mo   Cloth   25 cents each

Macaulay's Lays of Ancient Rome.
Macaulay's Life of Samuel Johnson.
Malory's Le Morte d'Arthur.
Milton's Comus and Other Poems.
Milton's Paradise Lost, Books I. and II.
Old English Ballads.
Old Testament (Selections from).
Out of the Northland.
Palgrave's Golden Treasury.
Parkman's Oregon Trail.
Plutarch's Lives (Cæsar, Brutus, and Mark Antony).
Poe's Poems.
Poe's Prose Tales (Selections from).
Poems, Narrative and Lyrical.
Pope's Homer's Iliad.
Pope's Homer's Odyssey.
Pope's The Rape of the Lock.
Ruskin's Sesame and Lilies.
Ruskin's The Crown of Wild Olive and Queen of the Air.
Scott's Ivanhoe.
Scott's Kenilworth.
Scott's Lady of the Lake.
Scott's Lay of the Last Minstrel.
Scott's Marmion.
Scott's Quentin Durward.
Scott's The Talisman.
Select Orations.
Select Poems, for required reading in Secondary Schools.
Shakespeare's As You Like It.
Shakespeare's As You Like It (Tudor).
Shakespeare's Comedy of Errors (Tudor).
Shakespeare's Coriolanus (Tudor).
Shakespeare's Hamlet.
Shakespeare's Henry IV, Part I (Tudor)
Shakespeare's Henry V.
Shakespeare's Henry VI, Part I (Tudor).
Shakespeare's Henry VIII (Tudor).
Shakespeare's Julius Cæsar.
Shakespeare's King Lear.
Shakespeare's Macbeth.
Shakespeare's Macbeth (Tudor).
Shakespeare's A Midsummer Night's Dream.
Shakespeare's A Midsummer Night's Dream (Tudor).
Shakespeare's Merchant of Venice.
Shakespeare's Merchant of Venice (Tudor).
Shakespeare's Richard II.
Shakespeare's Romeo and Juliet (Tudor)
Shakespeare's The Tempest.
Shakespeare's Troilus and Cressida (Tudor).
Shakespeare's Twelfth Night.
Shelley and Keats: Poems.
Sheridan's The Rivals and The School for Scandal.
Southern Poets: Selections.
Southern Orators: Selections.
Spenser's Faerie Queene, Book I.
Stevenson's Kidnapped.
Stevenson's The Master of Ballantrae.
Stevenson's Travels with a Donkey, and An Inland Voyage.
Stevenson's Treasure Island.
Swift's Gulliver's Travels.
Tennyson's Idylls of the King.
Tennyson's In Memoriam.
Tennyson's The Princess.
Tennyson's Shorter Poems.
Thackeray's English Humourists.
Thackeray's Henry Esmond.
Thoreau's Walden.
Virgil's Æneid.
Washington's Farewell Address, and Webster's First Bunker Hill Oration.
Whittier's Snow-Bound and Other Early Poems.
Woolman's Journal.
Wordsworth's Shorter Poems.

THE MACMILLAN COMPANY
NEW YORK · BOSTON · CHICAGO
SAN FRANCISCO

MACMILLAN & CO., Limited
LONDON · BOMBAY · CALCUTTA
MELBOURNE

THE MACMILLAN CO. OF CANADA, Ltd.
TORONTO

INTRODUCTION

These seven poems represent fairly well the poetry of the early and middle nineteenth century. They are here printed in the order of their original publication. Excepting *The Ancient Mariner*, they all appeared within the quarter-century between 1840 and 1865. It was in just this period, too, that Tennyson and Browning wrote their best poems.

But between 1798 and 1842 another great group, or rather series, of poets had earned a just and lasting fame. Coleridge is their only direct representative in this book. The others were Wordsworth and Keats and Shelley and Byron and Scott; and they are all indirectly represented here, for they left their stamp on the poetry that followed, and indeed on all poetry that has been written since. Wordsworth has special claim to mention here. He was joint author of the *Lyrical Ballads*, in which *The Ancient Mariner* appeared, and which marked a step in the development of English poetry.

In the great day of Shakespeare, poetry had been a living and free thing. By the beginning of the eighteenth century it had grown tame and artificial. It was still salable — Pope made a respectable fortune out of his verses. But in his hands English poetry would have died, if a racial poetry could ever die. He himself was a poet in spite of himself and his little rules. But in his own day he was supposed to be a very great poet because of them. The consequence was that for nearly a century everybody who wrote English verse tried to write like Pope. They succeeded, so far as the rules could carry them; but it was a sorry day for poetry, if poetry means anything more than a set jingle. Even Goldsmith, true poet that he was, did not dream of breaking away from Pope's rules. *The Traveller* and *The Deserted Village* are beautiful in spite of the measure in which they were written — or rather they triumph over that measure, and make it a beautiful thing in itself. In Goldsmith, and, shortly after him, in Burns and Cowper and Blake and Landor, poetry had begun to live again. So that when Coleridge and Wordsworth came to put forth the *Lyrical Ballads*, they were conscious champions of a new faith.

COLERIDGE AND WORDSWORTH

Samuel Taylor Coleridge and William Wordsworth met in 1796. Coleridge was twenty-four, Wordsworth two years older. Both had studied at the University of Cambridge, both had become enthusiasts in the revolutionary cause which absorbed all Europe and America at that time. They were very different in character, but both wished to be poets, and poets of a new order. Coleridge himself has given an account of the way in which they came to write the *Lyrical Ballads*: —

"During the first year Mr. Wordsworth and I were neighbours, our conversations turned frequently on the two cardinal points of poetry, the power of exciting the sympathy of the reader by a faithful adherence to the truth of nature, and the power of giving the interest of novelty by the modifying colours of imagination. The sudden charm, which accidents of light and shade, which moonlight or sunset, diffused over a known and familiar landscape, appeared to represent the practicability of combining both. These are the poetry of nature. The thought suggested itself (to which of us I do not recollect) that a series of poems might be composed of two sorts. In the one, the incidents and agents were to be, in part at least, supernatural; and the excellence aimed at was to consist in the interesting of the affections by the dramatic truth of such emotions as would naturally accompany such situations, supposing them real. And real in this sense they have been to every human being who, from whatever source of delusion, has at any time believed himself under supernatural agency. For the second class, subjects were to be chosen from ordinary life; the characters and incidents were to be such as will be found in every village and its vicinity where there is a meditative and feeling mind to seek after them, or to notice them when they present themselves.

"In this idea originated the plan of the 'Lyrical Ballads'; in which it was agreed that my endeavours should be directed to persons and characters supernatural, or at least romantic; yet so as to transfer from our inward nature a human interest and a semblance of truth sufficient to procure for these shadows of imagination that willing suspension of disbelief for the moment, which constitutes poetic faith. Mr. Wordsworth, on the other hand, was to propose to himself as his object, to give the charm of novelty to things of every day, and to excite a feeling analogous to the supernatural, by awakening the mind's attention from the lethargy of custom, and directing it to the loveliness and the wonders of the world before us; an inexhaustible treasure, but for which, in consequence of the film of familiarity and selfish solicitude, we have eyes, yet see not, ears that hear not, and hearts that neither feel nor understand."

INTRODUCTION

There were twenty-three poems in the *Lyrical Ballads*, of which Coleridge wrote only four; but *The Ancient Mariner* was one of them. The origin of this poem is described by Wordsworth in his *Memoirs:* —

"In the autumn of 1797 he (Coleridge), my sister, and myself, started from Alfoxden pretty late in the afternoon with a view to visit Linton and the Valley of Stones near to it. Accordingly we set off, and proceeded along the Quantock Hills towards Watchet, and in the course of this walk was planned the poem of *The Ancient Mariner*, founded on a dream, as Mr. Coleridge said, of his friend, Mr. Cruikshank. Much the greater part of the story was Mr. Coleridge's invention, but certain parts I suggested; for example, some crime was to be committed which should bring upon the Old Navigator, as Coleridge afterwards delighted to call him, the spectral persecution, as a consequence of that crime and his own wanderings. I had been reading in Shelvocke's *Voyages* a day or two before, that, while doubling Cape Horn, they frequently saw albatrosses in that latitude, the largest sort of sea-fowl, some extending their wings twelve or thirteen feet. 'Suppose,' said I, 'you represent him as having killed one of these birds on entering the South Sea, and that the tutelary spirits of these regions take upon them to avenge the crime.' The incident was thought fit for the purpose, and adopted accordingly. I also suggested the navigation of the ship by the dead men, but do not recollect that I had anything more to do with the scheme of the poem. The gloss with which it was subsequently accompanied was not thought of by either of us at the time, at least not a hint of it was given to me, and I have no doubt it was a gratuitous afterthought. We began the composition together on that, to me, memorable evening. I furnished two or three lines at the beginning of the poem, in particular: —

> ' And listen'd like a three years' child:
> The Mariner had his will.'

These trifling contributions, all but one, which Mr. Coleridge has with unnecessary scrupulosity recorded, slipped out of his mind, as they well might. As we endeavoured to proceed conjointly (I speak of the same evening), our respective manners proved so widely different that it would have been quite presumptuous in me to do anything but separate from an undertaking upon which I could only have been a clog."

Coleridge wrote much poetry, but his fame rests upon *The Ancient Mariner* and two other poems, *Christabel* and *Kubla Khan*, — each a marvel of its kind, and each with something strange and haunting in its beauty.

MACAULAY AND THE LAYS

Nearly half a century passed between the publication of *The Ancient Mariner* and the appearance of *The Lays of Ancient Rome*. In the meantime the new poetry, the poetry of naturalness as contrasted with the poetry of artifice, had been generally accepted. Instead of restricting themselves to one manner, as the eighteenth century versifiers had done, the early nineteenth century poets used a variety of forms. The old "poetic diction," — the set phrases and conventional images of the past, — was abandoned for the most part. Byron and Wordsworth, so different in most ways, were alike in their bold use of the English of common speech. Keats and Shelley strove for the free and irregular beauty which was the goal of the whole "romantic" movement, as it has come to be called. Unrhymed or "blank" verse, so flexible an instrument in the hands of the Elizabethans and of Milton, almost displaced the "heroic verse" — the regular rhymed couplets — of Pope and his clan.

Near the end of the eighteenth century the first collection of English and Scottish ballads was made by Bishop Percy. This natural and spontaneous poetry of the people had great influence upon the new poets. *The Ancient Mariner* has the form and flavor of an old ballad. Sir Walter Scott was saturated with this ancient ballad-literature, and all of his poetry is based upon it. *Marmion* and *The Lady of the Lake* are hardly more than ballads on a large scale. These two poems were published and became at once popular when Macaulay was a boy, and his Roman ballads, or lays, though they were not written till many years later, very clearly show the influence of Scott's style.

Macaulay was born in 1800, and the *Lays of Ancient Rome* were published in 1842. Long before then, he had distinguished himself as an essayist and a statesman. He entered Parliament at thirty, and was a member of the Supreme Council for India at thirty-four. His essays had made him famous as a writer. They were collected and published in the year after the *Lays* were printed. A few years later the famous *History of England* appeared, with extraordinary success. It sold like the *Waverley Novels*, and brought Macaulay a fortune and a title.

The sources of the *Lays* Macaulay has very fully described in his general and special prefaces, which ought by all means to be read in connection with the poems: —

"The early history of Rome," he says in the general Preface, "is far more poetical than anything else in Latin literature. The loves of the Vestal and the God of War, the cradle laid among the reeds of Tiber, the fig tree, the she-wolf, the shepherd's cabin, the recognition, the fratricide, the rape of the Sabines, the death of Tarpeia, the fall of Hostus Hostilius, the struggle of Mettus Curtius through the marsh, the women rushing with torn raiment and dishevelled hair between their fathers and their husbands, the nightly meetings of Numa and the Nymph by the well in the sacred grove, the fight of the three Romans and the three Albans, the purchase of the Sibylline books, the crime of Tullia, the simulated madness of Brutus, the ambiguous reply of the Delphian oracle to the Tarquins, the wrongs of Lucretia, the heroic actions of Horatius Cocles, of Scævola, and of Clœlia, the battle of Regillus won by the aid of Castor and Pollux, the defence of Cremera, the touching story of Coriolanus, the still more touching story of Virginia, the wild legend about the draining of the Alban lake, the combat between Valerius Corvus and the gigantic Gaul, are among the many instances which will at once suggest themselves to every reader."

Such themes as these, Macaulay believes, were treated by ballad-poets among the early Romans. The ballads have perished, and he has tried to reconstruct some of them: —

"In the following poems, the author speaks, not in his own person, but in the persons of ancient minstrels who know only what a Roman citizen, born three or four hundred years before the Christian era, may be supposed to have known, and who are in no wise above the passions and prejudices of their age and nation. To these imaginary poets must be ascribed some blunders which are so obvious that it is unnecessary to point them out. The real blunder would have been to represent these old poets as deeply versed in general history, and studious of chronological accuracy. To them must also be attributed the illiberal sneers at the Greeks, the furious party-spirit, the contempt for the arts of peace, the love of war for its own sake, the ungenerous exultation over the vanquished, which the reader will sometimes observe. To portray a Roman of the age of Camillus or Curius as superior to national antipathies, as mourning over the devastation and slaughter by which empire and triumphs were to be won, as looking on human suffering with the sympathy of Howard, or as treating conquered enemies with the delicacy of the Black Prince, would be to violate all dramatic propriety. The old Romans had some great virtues, fortitude, temperance, veracity, spirit to resist oppression, respect for legitimate authority, fidelity in the observing of contracts, disinterestedness, ardent patriotism; but Christian charity and chivalrous generosity were alike unknown to them.

"It would have been obviously improper to mimic the manner of any particular age or country. Something has been borrowed, however, from our own old ballads, and more from Sir Walter Scott, the great restorer of our ballad-poetry. To the *Iliad* still greater obligations are due; and those obligations have been contracted with the less hesitation, because there is reason to believe that some of the old Latin minstrels really had recourse to that inexhaustible store of poetical images."

Macaulay was not a poet of the first order, but in the *Lays*, and in a few other stirring poems, such as *Ivry* and *The Battle of Naseby*, he won a real and living success.

POE AND THE RAVEN

Poe had much more in common with Coleridge than with Macaulay. Macaulay was a man of practical ability as well as of genius. His life was a long series of social and material successes. Poe, like Coleridge, was comparatively unstable in character and purpose, and had a hard struggle of it. The bulk of his poetry, like Coleridge's, was small, and its quality strange. Poe chanced to be born in America a generation later than Coleridge, but there is nothing distinctively American about *The Raven*, as there is nothing distinctively English about *The Ancient Mariner*. The imagination of Poe, like the imagination of Coleridge, dwelt in No-man's-land, among cloudlike shadows, and dim images of mystery, or horror, or unearthly beauty.

Edgar Allan Poe was born in Boston in 1809, which was also the birth-year of Tennyson, Lincoln, and Holmes. He was brought up in the South, and was Southern rather than Northern in temperament and sympathies. He only lived to be forty years old, and his life was an unhappy one, partly by his own fault, and partly because it was then so hard, even for a man of combined genius and industry, to make a living with his pen. Coleridge was pensioned, early in life, by two rich patrons. Macaulay had independent means. But Poe, after being rather spoiled by his adopted father throughout boyhood, was cast suddenly upon his own resources. His early marriage to an invalid increased his burden, and his inherited bodily weaknesses and moral irresolution made that burden too heavy to be borne through a long career.

Poe's poetry, all that is best of it, is in a single key and within a narrow register, —

"A strange, a weird, a melancholy strain,
Like the low moaning of the distant sea."

The thought of death, especially of the death of youth and beauty, at once oppresses and inspires him. The result is a series of poems, very brief most of them, distinguished by a peculiar haunting melody. It is this singing quality which led Tennyson to pronounce Poe the best of American poets: "not unworthy to stand beside Catullus, the most melodious of Latins, and Heine, the most tuneful of Germans."

The Raven is the most popular if not the most beautiful of his poems. There are several accounts of its origin. One is that he wrote it in a few hours one night, to get money to buy medicines for his sick young wife. Another is that it was written bit by bit and submitted to various friends, who made suggestions, some of which were taken. Poe himself, in his paper called *The Philosophy of Composition*, has provided a queer account of his method of composing the poem. If it is true, neither of the other stories can have much truth in them. It would make out *The Raven* to be a very elaborate composition. Like most of Poe's poetry, it underwent a good deal of revision after its first publication.

Poe was confessedly a poet of sound. He despised preaching in verse, and declared that poetry is "the rhythmical creation of beauty." In *The Philosophy of Composition* he fully explains why his favorite theme is the naturally inspiring theme for him.

The highest note of beauty, he says, is sadness. The

beauty of woman is the perfect beauty, and her loss the irreparable loss: her death, therefore, "the most poetical topic in the world." "Upon it," says Woodberry, "he would lavish his impassioned music, heightening its effects by every metrical device, and by contrast with something of the quaint and grotesque — as the loveliness and glory of a mediæval structure are intensified by gargoyles, and by weird discordant tracery here and there. The greater part of Poe's verse accords with his theory at large. Several of the later poems illustrate it in general and particular. *The Raven* bears out his *ex post facto* analysis to the smallest detail. We have the note of hopelessness, the brooding regret, the artistic value supported by richly romantic properties in keeping; the occasion follows the death of a woman beautiful and beloved; the sinister bird is an emblem of the irreparable, and its voice the sombre 'Nevermore.' Finally, the melody of this strange poem is a vocal dead-march, and so compulsive with its peculiar measure, its refrain and repetends, that in the end even the more critical yielded to its quaintness and fantasy, and accorded it a lasting place in literature."

During his life, Poe's work was more generously recognized abroad, especially in France, than in America.

Lowell and The Vision of Sir Launfal

The Vision of Sir Launfal was published in 1848, three years after *The Raven*. Lowell was then under thirty, but had already made a name for himself. He and all the later poets to be included in this book belonged to the Macaulay rather than to the Coleridge-Poe type. That is, they were all men of firm character and, in one way or another, of practical usefulness to the world. Their struggles were not chiefly with poverty, or with their own weaknesses, but with the problems of life and art as they present themselves to men of strong nature.

James Russell Lowell was born in 1819, in the little village of Cambridge. His life was the life of a country boy. Harvard College was near by, and Lowell naturally entered there when the time came. Literature was a chief interest among college students in that day, when athletics did not exist, and there were few outside distractions. Lowell's fellow-undergraduates prophesied literary success for him — a prophecy which is often made in college, but does not always come true. When he was graduated, he promised his father to "give up poetry and go to work"; and he actually studied law for a time. But the writing instinct was too strong for him, and it was not long before he took to his pen in earnest. For some years he had to work hard, but not painfully; and he was still a young man when he became known both as poet and as prose-writer.

The Vision of Sir Launfal was written at a time when his imagination was particularly active. It is said to have been composed almost at a heat. Lowell, who was New England bred as well as New England born, did not share Poe's prejudice against preaching in verse. *The Vision* is very distinctly a poem with a moral. As it happens, this moral is very much like that of *The Ancient Mariner*. The Mariner's trouble begins when he wrongs one of God's creatures; Sir Launfal's begins when he scorns a poor beggar in his heart. And the cure is the same in both cases — the opening of the heart toward even the humblest of one's fellow-creatures. *The Vision* also expresses the mystical side of that double nature which Lowell recognized as his own: *The Fable for Critics*, that brilliant satire, had appeared a very short time before *The Vision of Sir Launfal*. One poem was as characteristic of Lowell as the other. It was at about the same date that he wrote to a friend: —

"I find myself very curiously compounded of two utterly distinct characters. One half of me is clear mystic and enthusiast, and the other humorist. If I had lived as solitary as a hermit of the Thebais, I doubt not that I should have had as authentic interviews with the Evil One as they, and, without any disrespect to the saint, it would have taken very little to have made a Saint Francis of me. Indeed, during that part of my life which I lived most alone, I was never a single night unvisited by visions, and once I thought I had a personal revelation from God himself. . . . On the other hand, had I mixed more with the world than I have, I should probably have become a Pantagruelist."

The visionary faculty finds expression in *Sir Launfal*. The poem is irregular in form, and Dr. Holmes rightly called Lowell's attention to its lack of finish and its incongruities. But it has a swing and enthusiasm that make up for minor faults. As Lowell's chief biographer says, "It has stood the test of time; it is beloved now by thousands of young American readers, for whom it has been a first initiation to the beauty of poetic idealism."

In simple poems like *The First Snow-Fall*, and in elaborate poems like the *Commemoration Ode*, Lowell has reached a higher level of poetic art; but none of his poems is more characteristic, in form and substance, than *The Vision of Sir Launfal*.

Arnold and Sohrab and Rustum

Matthew Arnold was a little younger than Lowell; he was born in 1822. His father was the famous Dr. Thomas Arnold of Rugby, and his mother was a remarkable woman. Arnold was a studious boy, and won poetical prizes both at Rugby and Oxford. After some experience as teacher and private secretary, he was made, at twenty-nine, an inspector of schools, and worked as inspector or commissioner for the rest of his life.

His fame as a writer, like Lowell's, has a double foundation. As critic and essayist he was acknowledged to be supreme in his generation. As a poet he has made his way more slowly in general esteem. He had not the qualities which made Tennyson and Browning popular, in their different ways, while they lived. There is something a little cold and remote about even his best work. He followed, that is, the classical models, and represents a reaction against the romantic tendency which led to such extravagances on the part of Browning and others among Arnold's contemporaries. On the other hand, he often fairly mounts to what he called "the grand style" — a style only to be approached by poets of a very high order.

INTRODUCTION   xxvii

These qualities of restraint and loftiness are well shown in *Sohrab and Rustum*. The poem appeared in the third collection of Arnold's poems. He was thirty-one years old when it was written, and the composition of it took hold of him in an uncommon way, as is shown by the following passage from a letter to his mother: —

"All my spare time has been spent on a poem which I have just finished, and which I think by far the best thing I have yet done, and I think it will be generally liked; though one can never be sure of this. I have had the greatest pleasure in composing it, a rare thing with me, and, as I think, a good test of the pleasure what you write is likely to afford to others. But the story is a very noble and excellent one."

There are several versions in English of the Persian legend of *Sohrab and Rustum*. The one upon which Arnold founded his poem is given in Sir John Malcolm's *History of Persia:* —

"The young Sohrab was the fruit of one of Rustum's early amours. He had left his mother, and sought fame under the banners of Afrasiab, whose armies he commanded. He had carried death and dismay into the ranks of the Persians, and had terrified the boldest warriors of that country, before Rustum encountered him, which at last that hero resolved to do. They met three times. The first time they parted by mutual consent, though Sohrab had the advantage; the second, the youth obtained a victory, but granted life to his unknown father; the third was fatal to Sohrab, who, when writhing in the pangs of death, warned the conqueror to shun the vengeance that is inspired by parental woes, and bade him dread the rage of the mighty Rustum, who must soon learn that he had slain his son Sohrab. These words, we are told, were as death to the aged hero, and when he recovered from a trance, he called in despair for proofs of what Sohrab had said. The afflicted and dying youth tore open his mail, and showed his father a seal which his mother had placed on his arm when she discovered to him the secret of his birth, and bade him seek his father. The sight of his own signet rendered Rustum quite frantic; he cursed himself, attempting to put an end to his existence, and was only prevented by the efforts of his expiring son. After Sohrab's death, he burnt his tents and all his goods, and carried the corpse to Seistan, where it was interred; the army of Turan was, agreeably to the last request of Sohrab, permitted to cross the Oxus unmolested. To reconcile us to the improbability of the tale, we are informed that Rustum could have no idea that his son was in existence. The mother of Sohrab had written to him her child was a daughter, fearing to lose her darling infant if she revealed the truth; and Rustum fought under a feigned name, an usage not uncommon to the chivalrous combats of those days."

Longfellow and The Courtship of Miles Standish

Longfellow was born in 1807. He was therefore past middle age when, in 1858, *The Courtship of Miles Standish* was published. He had been putting forth poetry for twenty years, and had produced much of his best. His earliest work, like that of most poets, was imitative, and had little about it that was distinctively American. But in 1847 appeared *Evangeline*, in subject a new-world poem. Oddly enough, it was cast in one of the most ancient of moulds, the metre of Homer and Virgil. It is not a metre which is naturally adapted to the English tongue. Our language is made up of short, choppy words, while the dactylic measure of the *Iliad* or the *Æneid* is built of long, rolling words, many of them with unaccented inflectional endings. Only a few poems of any account have been written in this measure in English. Two of them, *Evangeline*, and *The Courtship of Miles Standish* which followed eleven years later, are Longfellow's.

Henry Wadsworth Longfellow was born in Portland, Maine. He studied at Bowdoin College in the remarkable class which also contained Hawthorne. Like Lowell, he made up his mind to gain success as a writer, and like Lowell, he became a professor at Harvard, and lived a life in which money troubles played no part. Indeed, his whole career was so sheltered and so uniformly successful, that we must think of him as one of the most enviable among literary men. His poetry has the serene quiet strength which might be expected to be the fruit of such a life. It is not brilliant or enchanting, but it is sound and sweet.

Longfellow's diary gives account of the writing of *The Courtship of Miles Standish*: —

December 2, 1857. "Soft as spring. I begin a new poem, *Priscilla;* to be a kind of Puritan pastoral; the subject, the courtship of Miles Standish. This, I think, will be a better treatment of the subject than the dramatic one I wrote some time ago."

December 3d, 1857. "My poem is in hexameters, an idyl of the Old Colony times."

December 29th, 1857. "Wrote a little at *Priscilla*."

January 29th, 1858. "Began again on *Priscilla*, and wrote several pages, finishing the second canto."

February 17, 1858. "Have worked pretty steadily for the last week on *Priscilla*. To-day finish canto four."

March 1, 1858. "Keep indoors, and work on *Priscilla*, which I think I shall call *The Courtship of Miles Standish*."

March 16, 1858. "But I find time, notwithstanding, to write a whole canto of *Miles Standish*, namely, canto eight."

March 22d. "The poem is finished, and now only needs revision, which I begin to-day. But in the main, I have it as I want it."

April 23d. "Printing *Miles Standish*, and seeing all its defects as it stands before me in type."

The book did not appear till October. On the 16th of that month the following entry was made: —

"*The Courtship of Miles Standish* published. At noon Ticknor told me he had sold five thousand in Boston, besides the orders from a distance. He had printed ten thousand, and has another ten thousand in press." On the 23rd he wrote, "Between these two Saturdays, *Miles Standish* has marched steadily on. Another five thousand are in press; in all an army of twenty-five thousand, — in one week. Fields tells me that in London ten thousand were sold the first day."

WHITTIER AND SNOW-BOUND

Whittier's birth-year was the same as Longfellow's, and their reputations grew side by side. They became the most popular American poets abroad as well as in America. "This parallelism in their fame makes it the more interesting to remember that Whittier was born within five miles of the Longfellow homestead, where the grandfather of his brother poet was born. Always friends, though never intimate, they represented through life two quite different modes of rearing and education. Longfellow was the most widely travelled author of the Boston circle, Whittier the least so; Longfellow spoke a variety of languages, Whittier only his own; Longfellow had whatever the American college of his time could give him, Whittier had none of it; Longfellow had the habits of a man of the world, Whittier those of a recluse; Longfellow touched reform but lightly, Whittier was essentially imbued with it; Longfellow had children and grandchildren, while Whittier led a single life. Yet in certain gifts, apart from poetic quality, they were alike; both being modest, serene, unselfish, brave, industrious, and generous. They either shared, or made up between them, many of the most estimable qualities that mark poet or man."[1]

Whittier was a boy of the farm, Longfellow of the town. *Snow-Bound* is a memory of country joys as serene and beautiful in its way as *The Cotter's Saturday Night* or *The Deserted Village*. Whittier has been called the

[1] *A Reader's History of American Literature*, by T. W. Higginson and H. W. Boynton.

Burns of America. We know that a volume of Burns first awoke his poetic ambition; and it is certain that he is our greatest singer. Even Longfellow "composed poems," while Whittier burst spontaneously and sometimes rudely into song.

The scene of *Snow-Bound* can easily be visited. The Whittier homestead in East Haverhill has been bought and restored, and is to be kept as a memorial of the poet. Even the old furniture of his boyhood has much of it been returned to its place. The persons of the poem are the members of Whittier's own family, the district school-teacher, and another guest who had made a strong impression on the boy's imagination.

Whittier's family were Quakers, and he disbelieved in war. But his was a fighting spirit, and much of his early verse was written against slavery. When the Civil War broke out, his voice could not be silent. But it is in poems like *Snow-Bound*, poems of his own place and his own people, that his voice is clearest and sweetest.

THE RIME
OF THE ANCIENT MARINER

IN SEVEN PARTS

Facile credo, plures esse Naturas invisibiles quam visibiles in rerum universitate. Sed horum omnium familiam quis nobis enarrabit? et gradus et cognationes et discrimina et singulorum munera? Quid agunt? quæ loca habitant? Harum rerum notitiam semper ambivit ingenium humanum, nunquam attigit. Juvat, interea, non diffiteor, quandoque in animo, tanquam in tabulâ, majoris et melioris mundi imaginem contemplari: ne mens assuefacta hodiernæ vitæ minutiis se contrahat nimis, et tota subsidat in pusillas cogitationes. Sed veritati interea invigilandum est, modusque servandus, ut certa ab incertis, diem a nocte, distinguamus. — T. BURNET, *Archæol. Phil.*, p. 68.

ARGUMENT

How a Ship having passed the Line was driven by storms to the cold Country towards the South Pole: and how from thence she made her course to the tropical Latitude of the Great Pacific Ocean; and of the strange things that befell; and in what manner the Ancyent Marinere came back to his own Country. (1798.)

PART I

It° is an ancient Mariner, An ancient Mariner meeteth three Gallants bidden to a wedding-feast, and detaineth one.
   And he stoppeth one of three.
" By thy long grey beard and glittering eye,
   Now wherefore stopp'st thou me?

The Bridegroom's doors are opened wide,
   And I am next of kin;
The guests are met, the feast is set:
   May'st hear the merry din."

He° holds him with his skinny hand,
   "There was a ship," quoth he.
"Hold off! unhand me, grey-beard loon!"
   Eftsoons° his hand dropt he.

The Wedding-Guest is spellbound by the eye of the old sea-faring man, and constrained to hear his tale.

He holds him with his glittering eye —
   The Wedding-Guest stood still,
And listens like a three years' child:
   The Mariner hath his will.

The Wedding-Guest sat on a stone:
   He cannot choose but hear;
And thus spake on that ancient man,
   The bright-eyed Mariner.

"The ship was cheered, the harbour cleared,
   Merrily did we drop
Below the kirk, below the hill,
   Below the lighthouse top.

The Sun came up upon the left,° 25
  Out of the sea came he!
And he shone bright, and on the right
  Went down into the sea.

Higher and higher every day,
  Till over the mast at noon° —" 30
The Wedding-Guest here beat his breast,°
  For he heard the loud bassoon.

The Mariner tells how the ship sailed southward with a good wind and fair weather, till it reached the Line.

The bride hath paced into the hall,
  Red as a rose is she;
Nodding their heads before her goes 35
  The merry minstrelsy.

The Wedding-Guest heareth the bridal music; but the Mariner continueth his tale.

The Wedding-Guest he beat his breast,
  Yet he cannot choose but hear;
And thus spake on that ancient man,
  The bright-eyed Mariner. 40

"And now the Storm-blast came, and he
  Was tyrannous and strong:
He struck with his o'ertaking wings,
  And chased us south along.

The ship drawn by a storm toward the south pole.

SELECTED POEMS

With sloping masts and dipping prow, 45
As who pursued with yell and blow
Still treads the shadow of his foe,
   And forward bends his head,
The ship drove fast, loud roared the blast,
   And southward aye we fled. 50

And now there came both mist and snow,
   And it grew wondrous cold:
And ice, mast-high, came floating by,
   As green as emerald.

The land of ice, and of fearful sounds where no living thing was to be seen.

And through the drifts the snowy clifts 55
   Did send a dismal sheen:
Nor shapes of men nor beasts we ken —
   The ice was all between.

The ice was here, the ice was there,
   The ice was all around: 60
It cracked and growled, and roared and howled,
   Like noises in a swound°!

Till a great sea-bird, called the Albatross, came through the snow-fog, and was received with great joy and hospitality.

At length did cross an Albatross,
   Thorough° the fog it came;
As if it had been a Christian soul, 65
   We hailed it in God's name.

It ate the food it ne'er had eat,
  And round and round it flew.
The ice did split with a thunder-fit°;
  The helmsman steered us through! 70

And a good south wind sprung up behind; *And lo! the Albatross proveth a bird of good omen, and followeth the ship as it returned northward through fog and floating ice.*
  The Albatross did follow,
And every day, for food or play,
  Came to the mariner's hollo!

In mist or cloud, on mast or shroud, 75
  It perched for vespers nine;
Whiles all the night, through fog-smoke white,
  Glimmered the white moon-shine."

"God save thee,° ancient Mariner, 79 *The ancient Mariner inhospitably killeth the pious bird of good omen.*
  From the fiends, that plague thee thus!—
Why look'st thou so?"—"With my cross-bow
  I shot the Albatross.

Part II

The Sun now rose upon the right.°
  Out of the sea came he,

SELECTED POEMS

Still hid in mist, and on the left 85
    Went down into the sea.

And the good south wind still blew behind,
    But no sweet bird did follow,
Nor any day for food or play
    Came to the mariner's hollo! 90

His shipmates cry out against the ancient Mariner, for killing the bird of good luck.

And I had done a hellish thing,
    And it would work 'em woe:
For all averred, I had killed the bird
    That made the breeze to blow.
Ah wretch! said they, the bird to slay, 95
    That made the breeze to blow!

But when the fog cleared off, they justify the same, and thus make themselves accomplices in the crime.

Nor dim nor red, like God's own head
    The glorious Sun uprist:
Then all averred, I had killed the bird
    That brought the fog and mist. 100
'Twas right, said they, such birds to slay,
    That bring the fog and mist.

The fair breeze continues; the ship enters the Pacific Ocean, and sails northward, even till it reaches the Line.

The fair breeze blew, the white foam flew,
    The furrow followed free;
We were the first that ever burst 105
    Into that silent sea!

Down dropt the breeze, the sails dropt down,   *The ship hath been suddenly becalmed.*
  'Twas sad as sad could be;
And we did speak only to break
  The silence of the sea!   110

All in a hot and copper sky,
  The bloody Sun, at noon,
Right up above the mast did stand,
  No bigger than the Moon.

Day after day, day after day,   115
  We stuck, nor breath nor motion;
As idle as a painted ship
  Upon a painted ocean.

Water, water, everywhere,   *And the Albatross begins to be avenged.*
  And all the boards did shrink;   120
Water, water, everywhere,
  Nor any drop to drink.

The very deep did rot: O Christ!
  That ever this should be!
Yea, slimy things did crawl with legs   125
  Upon the slimy sea.

SELECTED POEMS

About, about, in reel and rout
    The death-fires° danced at night;
The water, like a witch's oils,
    Burnt green, and blue, and white.   130

And some in dreams assured were
    Of the spirit that plagued us so;
Nine fathom deep he had followed us
    From the land of mist and snow.

And every tongue, through utter drought,
    Was withered at the root;   136
We could not speak, no more than if
    We had been choked with soot.

Ah! well-a-day! what evil looks
    Had I from old and young!   140
Instead of the cross, the Albatross
    About my neck was hung.

PART III

There passed a weary time. Each throat
    Was parched, and glazed each eye.
A weary time! a weary time!   145
    How glazed each weary eye,

Marginal glosses:

A Spirit had followed them; one of the invisible inhabitants of this planet, neither departed souls nor angels; concerning whom the learned Jew, Josephus, and the Platonic Constantinopolitan, Michael Psellus, may be consulted. They are very numerous, and there is no climate or element without one or more.

The shipmates, in their sore distress, would fain throw the whole guilt on the ancient Mariner; in sign whereof they hang the dead sea-bird round his neck.

THE RIME OF THE ANCIENT MARINER 9

When looking westward, I beheld
  A something in the sky.

The ancient Mariner beholdeth a sign in the element afar off.

At first it seemed a little speck,
  And then it seemed a mist; 150
It moved and moved, and took at last
  A certain shape, I wist.

A speck, a mist, a shape, I wist!
  And still it neared and neared:
As if it dodged a water-sprite, 155
  It plunged and tacked and veered.

With throats unslaked, with black lips baked,
  We could nor laugh nor wail;
Through utter drought all dumb we stood!
I bit my arm, I sucked the blood, 160
  And cried, A sail, a sail!

At its nearer approach, it seemeth him to be a ship; and at a dear ransom he freeth his speech from the bonds of thirst.

With throats unslaked, with black lips baked,
  Agape they heard me call:
Gramercy! they for joy did grin,°
And all at once their breath drew in, 165
  As they were drinking all.

A flash of joy;

And horror follows. For can it be a ship that comes onward without wind or tide?

See! see! (I cried) she tacks no more!
  Hither to work us weal;
Without a breeze, without a tide,
  She steadies with upright keel! 170

The western wave was all a-flame,
  The day was well-nigh done!
Almost upon the western wave
  Rested the broad bright Sun;
When that strange shape drove suddenly
  Betwixt us and the Sun. 176

It seemeth him but the skeleton of a ship.

And straight the Sun was flecked with bars,
  (Heaven's Mother send us grace!)
As if through a dungeon-grate he peered
  With broad and burning face. 180

Alas! (thought I, and my heart beat loud)
  How fast she nears and nears!
Are those her sails that glance in the Sun,
  Like restless gossameres?

And its ribs are seen as bars on the face of the setting Sun.

Are those her ribs through which the Sun
  Did peer, as through a grate? 186
And is that Woman all her crew?

Is that a Death° and are there two? The Spectre-Woman and her Death-mate, and no other on board the skeleton ship.
  Is Death that Woman's mate?

Her lips were red, her looks were free, 190
  Her locks were yellow as gold: Like vessel, like crew!
Her skin was as white as leprosy,
The Night-mare Life-in-Death was she,
  Who thicks man's blood with cold.

The naked hulk alongside came, 195 Death and Life-in-Death have diced for the ship's crew, and she (the latter) winneth the ancient Mariner.
  And the twain were casting dice;
'The game is done! I've won! I've won!'
  Quoth she, and whistles thrice.

The Sun's rim dips; the stars rush out: No twilight within the courts of the Sun.
  At one stride comes the dark; 200
With far-heard whisper, o'er the sea,
  Off shot the spectre-bark.

We listened and looked sideways up! At the rising of the Moon,
Fear at my heart, as at a cup,
  My life-blood seemed to sip! 205
The stars were dim, and thick the night,
The steersman's face by his lamp gleamed white;
  From the sails the dew did drip —

SELECTED POEMS

    Till clomb above the eastern bar
    The horned Moon, with one bright star 210
      Within the nether tip.°

One after another,

    One after one, by the star-dogged Moon,
      Too quick for groan or sigh,
    Each turned his face with a ghastly pang,
      And cursed me with his eye.   215

His shipmates drop down dead.

    Four times fifty living men,
      (And I heard nor sigh nor groan)
    With heavy thump, a lifeless lump,
      They dropped down one by one.

But Life-in-Death begins her work on the ancient Mariner.

    The souls did from their bodies fly, — 220
      They fled to bliss or woe!
    And every soul, it passed me by,
      Like the whizz of my cross-bow°!"

Part IV

The Wedding-Guest feareth that a Spirit is talking to him;

    " I fear thee, ancient Mariner!
      I fear thy skinny hand!   225
    And thou art long, and lank, and brown,
      As is the ribbed sea-sand.

THE RIME OF THE ANCIENT MARINER 13

I fear thee and thy glittering eye,
    And thy skinny hand, so brown." —
" Fear not, fear not, thou Wedding-Guest !
    This body dropt not down.   231

But the ancient Mariner assureth him of his bodily life, and proceedeth to relate his horrible penance.

Alone, alone, all, all alone,
    Alone on a wide wide sea !
And never a saint took pity on
    My soul in agony.   235

The many men, so beautiful !
    And they all dead did lie :
And a thousand thousand slimy things
    Lived on ; and so did I.

He despiseth the creatures of the calm.

I looked upon the rotting sea,   240
    And drew my eyes away ;
I looked upon the rotting deck,
    And there the dead men lay.

And envieth that they should live, and so many lie dead.

I looked to Heaven, and tried to pray ;
    But or ever a prayer had gusht,   245
A wicked whisper came, and made
    My heart as dry as dust.

I closed my lids, and kept them close,
　　And the balls like pulses beat;
For the sky and the sea, and the sea and the
　　　　sky
Lay like a load on my weary eye,
　　And the dead were at my feet.

But the curse liveth for him in the eye of the dead men.

The cold sweat melted from their limbs,
　　Nor rot nor reek did they:
The look with which they looked on me
　　Had never passed away.

An orphan's curse would drag to Hell
　　A spirit from on high;
But oh! more horrible than that
　　Is a curse in a dead man's eye!
Seven days, seven nights, I saw that curse,
　　And yet I could not die.

In his loneliness and fixedness he yearneth towards the journeying Moon, and the stars that still sojourn, yet still move onward; and everywhere the blue sky belongs

The moving Moon went up the sky,
　　And no where did abide:
Softly she was going up,
　　And a star or two beside —

Her beams bemocked the sultry main,
　　Like April hoar-frost spread;

But where the ship's huge shadow lay,
The charmed water burnt alway   270
   A still and awful red.

Beyond the shadow of the ship,
   I watched the water-snakes:
They moved in tracks of shining white,
And when they reared, the elfish light 275
   Fell off in hoary flakes.

Within the shadow of the ship
   I watched their rich attire:
Blue, glossy green, and velvet black,
They coiled and swam; and every track
   Was a flash of golden fire.   281

O happy living things! no tongue
   Their beauty might declare:
A spring of love gushed from my heart,
   And I blessed them unaware: 285
Sure my kind saint took pity on me,
   And I blessed them unaware.

The selfsame moment I could pray;
   And from my neck so free

to them, and is their appointed rest, and their native country and their own natural homes, which they enter unannounced, as lords that are certainly expected and yet there is a silent joy at their arrival.

By the light of the Moon he beholdeth God's creatures of the great calm.

Their beauty and their happiness.

He blesseth them in his heart.

The spell begins to break.

> The Albatross fell off,° and sank 290
>   Like lead into the sea.

Part V

> Oh sleep! it is a gentle thing,
>   Beloved from pole to pole!
> To Mary Queen the praise be given!
> She sent the gentle sleep from Heaven, 295
>   That slid into my soul.

By grace of the holy Mother, the ancient Mariner is refreshed with rain.

> The silly° buckets on the deck,
>   That had so long remained,
> I dreamt that they were filled with dew;
>   And when I awoke, it rained. 300

> My lips were wet, my throat was cold,
>   My garments all were dank;
> Sure I had drunken in my dreams,
>   And still my body drank.

> I moved, and could not feel my limbs: 305
>   I was so light — almost
> I thought that I had died in sleep,
>   And was a blessed ghost.°

And soon I heard a roaring wind:
   It did not come anear;   310
But with its sound it shook the sails,
   That were so thin and sere.

He heareth sounds and seeth strange sights and commotions in the sky and the element.

The upper air burst into life!
   And a hundred fire-flags sheen,
To and fro they were hurried about!   315
And to and fro, and in and out,
   The wan stars danced between.

And the coming wind did roar more loud,
   And the sails did sigh like sedge;
And the rain poured down from one black
     cloud;   320
   The Moon was at its edge.

The thick black cloud was cleft, and still
   The Moon was at its side:
Like waters shot from some high crag,
The lightning fell with never a jag,   325
   A river steep and wide.

The loud wind never reached the ship,
   Yet now the ship moved on!

The bodies of the ship's crew

are inspired, and the ship moves on;

Beneath the lightning and the Moon
   The dead men gave a groan.   330

They groaned, they stirred, they all uprose,
   Nor spake, nor moved their eyes;
It had been strange, even in a dream,
   To have seen those dead men rise.
The helmsman steered, the ship moved on;
   Yet never a breeze up blew;   336

The mariners all 'gan work the ropes,
   Where they were wont to do;
They raised their limbs like lifeless tools —
   We were a ghastly crew.   340

The body of my brother's son
   Stood by me, knee to knee:
The body and I pulled at one rope,
   But he said nought to me."

But not by the souls of the men, nor by dæmons of earth or middle air, but by a blessed troop of angelic spirits, sent down by the invocation of the guardian saint.

" I fear thee, ancient Mariner!"   345
   " Be calm, thou Wedding-Guest!
'Twas not those souls that fled in pain,
Which to their corses came again,
   But a troop of spirits blest:

For when it dawned — they dropped their
    arms,   350
  And clustered round the mast;
Sweet sounds rose slowly through their
    mouths,
  And from their bodies passed.

Around, around, flew each sweet sound,
  Then darted to the Sun;   355
Slowly the sounds came back again,
  Now mixed, now one by one.

Sometimes a-dropping from the sky
  I heard the sky-lark sing;
Sometimes all little birds that are,   360
How they seemed to fill the sea and air
  With their sweet jargoning!

And now 'twas like all instruments,
  Now like a lonely flute;
And now it is an angel's song,   365
  That makes the Heavens be mute.

It ceased; yet still the sails made on
  A pleasant noise till noon,

SELECTED POEMS

A noise like of a hidden brook
  In the leafy month of June,   370
That to the sleeping woods all night
  Singeth a quiet tune.

Till noon we quietly sailed on,
  Yet never a breeze did breathe:
Slowly and smoothly went the ship,   375
  Moved onward from beneath.

The lonesome Spirit from the south-pole carries on the ship as far as the Line, in obedience to the angelic troop, but still requireth vengeance.

Under the keel nine fathom deep,
  From the land of mist and snow,
The Spirit slid: and it was he
  That made the ship to go.   380
The sails at noon left off their tune,
  And the ship stood still also.

The Sun, right up above the mast,
  Had fixed her to the ocean:
But in a minute she 'gan stir,   385
  With a short uneasy motion —
Backwards and forwards half her length,
  With a short uneasy motion.

Then like a pawing horse let go,
  She made a sudden bound: 390

THE RIME OF THE ANCIENT MARINER

It flung the blood into my head,
    And I fell down in a swound.

How long in that same fit I lay,
    I have not to declare,
But ere my living life returned,   395
I heard and in my soul discerned
    Two voices in the air.

'Is it he?' quoth one, 'Is this the man?
    By Him who died on cross,
With his cruel bow he laid full low   400
    The harmless Albatross.

The Spirit who bideth by himself
    In the land of mist and snow,
He loved the bird that loved the man
    Who shot him with his bow.'   405

The other was a softer voice,
    As soft as honey-dew:
Quoth he, 'The man hath penance done,
    And penance more will do.'

The Polar Spirit's fellow-dæmons, the invisible inhabitants of the element, take part in his wrong; and two of them relate, one to the other, that penance long and heavy for the ancient Mariner hath been accorded to the Polar Spirit, who returneth southward.

Part VI

First Voice

'But tell me, tell me! speak again,   410
  Thy soft response renewing —
What makes that ship drive on so fast?
  What is the ocean doing?'

Second Voice

'Still as a slave before his lord,
  The ocean hath no blast;   415
His great bright eye most silently
  Up to the Moon is cast —

If he may know which way to go;
  For she guides him smooth or grim.
See, brother, see! how graciously   420
  She looketh down on him.'

The Mariner hath been cast into a trance; for the angelic power causeth the vessel to drive northward faster than human life could endure.

First Voice

'But why drives on that ship so fast,
  Without or wave or wind?'

SECOND VOICE

' The air is cut away before,
   And closes from behind.

Fly, brother, fly! more high, more high!
   Or we shall be belated:
For slow and slow that ship will go,
   When the Mariner's trance is abated.'

I woke, and we were sailing on
   As in a gentle weather:
'Twas night, calm night, the Moon was high,
   The dead men stood together.

The supernatural motion is retarded; the Mariner awakes, and his penance begins anew.

All stood together on the deck,
   For a charnel-dungeon fitter:
All fixed on me their stony eyes,
   That in the Moon did glitter.

The pang, the curse, with which they died,
   Had never passed away:
I could not draw my eyes from theirs,
   Nor turn them up to pray.

24   SELECTED POEMS

The curse is finally expiated.

And now this spell was snapt: once more
   I viewed the ocean green,
And looked far forth, yet little saw
   Of what had else been seen —   445

Like one, that on a lonesome road
   Doth walk in fear and dread,
And, having once turned round, walks on,
   And turns no more his head;
Because he knows, a frightful fiend   450
   Doth close behind him tread.

But soon there breathed a wind on me,
   Nor sound nor motion made:
Its path was not upon the sea,
   In ripple or in shade.   455

It raised my hair, it fanned my cheek
   Like a meadow-gale of spring —
It mingled strangely with my fears,
   Yet it felt like a welcoming.

Swiftly, swiftly flew the ship,   460
   Yet she sailed softly too:
Sweetly, sweetly blew the breeze —
   On me alone it blew.

Oh! dream of joy°! is this indeed
   The lighthouse top I see?
Is this the hill? is this the kirk?
   Is this mine own countree?

And the ancient Mariner beholdeth his native country. 465

We drifted o'er the harbour-bar,
   And I with sobs did pray —
O let me be awake, my God! 470
   Or let me sleep alway.

The harbour-bay was clear as glass,
   So smoothly it was strewn!
And on the bay the moonlight lay,
   And the shadow of the Moon. 475

The rock shone bright, the kirk no less,
   That stands above the rock:
The moonlight steeped in silentness
   The steady weathercock.

And the bay was white with silent light,
   Till rising from the same, 481
Full many shapes, that shadows were,
   In crimson colours came.

The angelic spirits leave the dead bodies,

And appear in their own forms of light.

A little distance from the prow
  Those crimson shadows were: 485
I turned my eyes upon the deck —
  Oh, Christ! what saw I there!

Each corse lay flat, lifeless and flat,
  And, by the holy rood!
A man all light, a seraph-man,   490
  On every corse there stood.

This seraph-band, each waved his hand:
  It was a heavenly sight!
They stood as signals to the land,
  Each one a lovely light;   495

This seraph-band, each waved his hand,
  No voice did they impart —
No voice; but oh! the silence sank
  Like music on my heart.

But soon I heard the dash of oars,   500
  I heard the Pilot's cheer;
My head was turned perforce away,
  And I saw a boat appear.

THE RIME OF THE ANCIENT MARINER

The Pilot and the Pilot's boy,
  I heard them coming fast: 505
Dear Lord in Heaven! it was a joy
  The dead men could not blast.

I saw a third — I heard his voice:
  It is the Hermit good!
He singeth loud his godly hymns   510
  That he makes in the wood.
He'll shrieve my soul, he'll wash away
  The Albatross's blood.

Part VII

This Hermit good lives in that wood   *The Hermit of the Wood*
  Which slopes down to the sea.   515
How loudly his sweet voice he rears!
He loves to talk with marineres
  That come from a far countree.

He kneels at morn, and noon, and eve —
  He hath a cushion plump: 520
It is the moss that wholly hides
  The rotted old oak-stump.

The skiff-boat neared: I heard them talk,
  'Why, this is strange, I trow!
Where are those lights so many and fair,
  That signal made but now?'   526

Approacheth the ship with wonder.

'Strange, by my faith!' the Hermit said —
  'And they answered not our cheer!
The planks look warped! and see those sails,
  How thin they are and sere!   530
I never saw aught like to them,
  Unless perchance it were

Brown skeletons of leaves that lag
  My forest-brook along;
When the ivy-tod° is heavy with snow, 535
And the owlet whoops to the wolf below,
  That eats the she-wolf's young.'

'Dear Lord! it hath a fiendish look —
  (The Pilot made reply)
I am a-feared' — 'Push on, push on!' 540
  Said the Hermit cheerily.

The boat came closer to the ship,
  But I nor spake nor stirred;

THE RIME OF THE ANCIENT MARINER 29

The boat came close beneath the ship,
  And straight a sound was heard.   545

Under the water it rumbled on,   *The ship suddenly sinketh.*
  Still louder and more dread:
It reached the ship, it split the bay;
  The ship went down like lead.

Stunned by that loud and dreadful sound,   *The ancient Mariner is saved in the Pilot's boat.*
  Which sky and ocean smote,   551
Like one that hath been seven days drowned
  My body lay afloat;
But swift as dreams, myself I found
  Within the Pilot's boat.   555

Upon the whirl, where sank the ship,
  The boat spun round and round;
And all was still, save that the hill
  Was telling of the sound.

I moved my lips — the Pilot shrieked   560
  And fell down in a fit;
The holy Hermit raised his eyes,
  And prayed where he did sit.

I took the oars: the Pilot's boy,
　　Who now doth crazy go,　　　　　　　　565
Laughed loud and long, and all the while
　　His eyes went to and fro.
'Ha, ha!' quoth he, 'full plain I see,
　　The Devil knows how to row.'

And now, all in my own countree,　　　　570
　　I stood on the firm land!
The Hermit stepped forth from the boat,
　　And scarcely he could stand.

<small>The ancient Mariner earnestly entreateth the Hermit to shrieve him; and the penance of life falls on him.</small>

'O shrieve me, shrieve me, holy man!'
　　The Hermit crossed his brow,　　　　575
'Say quick,' quoth he, 'I bid thee say —
　　What manner of man art thou?'

Forthwith this frame of mine was wrenched
　　With a woful agony,
Which forced me to begin my tale;　　　580
　　And then it left me free.

<small>And ever and anon throughout his future life an agony constraineth him to travel from land to land,</small>

Since then, at an uncertain hour,
　　That agony returns;
And till my ghastly tale is told,
　　This heart within me burns.　　　　　585

I pass, like night, from land to land;
  I have strange power of speech;
That moment that his face I see,
I know the man that must hear me:
  To him my tale I teach.   590

What loud uproar bursts from that door!
  The wedding-guests are there:

But in the garden-bower the bride
  And bride-maids singing are:
And hark the little vesper bell,   595
  Which biddeth me to prayer!

O Wedding-Guest! this soul hath been
  Alone on a wide wide sea:
So lonely 'twas, that God himself
  Scarce seemed there to be.   600

O sweeter than the marriage-feast,
  'Tis sweeter far to me,
To walk together to the kirk
  With a goodly company! —

To walk together to the kirk,   605
  And all together pray,

While each to his great Father bends,
Old men, and babes, and loving friends,
 And youths and maidens gay!

And to teach, by his own example, love and reverence to all things that God made and loveth.

Farewell, farewell! but this I tell 610
 To thee, thou Wedding-Guest!
He prayeth well, who loveth well
 Both man and bird and beast.

He prayeth best, who loveth best
 All things both great and small; 615
For the dear God who loveth us,
 He made and loveth all."

The Mariner, whose eye is bright,
 Whose beard with age is hoar,
Is gone: and now the Wedding-Guest 620
 Turned from the bridegroom's door.

He went like one that hath been stunned,
 And is of sense forlorn:
A sadder and a wiser man,
 He rose the morrow morn. 625

LAYS OF ANCIENT ROME

HORATIUS

A LAY MADE ABOUT THE YEAR OF THE CITY CCCLX

I

Lars Porsena of Clusium
  By the Nine Gods he swore
That the great house of Tarquin°
  Should suffer wrong no more.
By the Nine Gods he swore it,　　　　　　　5
  And named a trysting day,
And bade his messengers ride forth,
East and west and south and north,
  To summon his array.

II

East and west and south and north　　　　10
  The messengers ride fast,
And tower and town and cottage
  Have heard the trumpet's blast.
Shame on the false Etruscan
  Who lingers in his home,　　　　　　　15
When Porsena of Clusium
  Is on the march for Rome.

III

The horsemen and the footmen
  Are pouring in amain
From many a stately market-place,
  From many a fruitful plain,
From many a lonely hamlet,
  Which, hid by beech and pine,
Like an eagle's nest, hangs on the crest
  Of purple Apennine;

IV

From lordly Volaterræ,
  Where scowls the far-famed hold
Piled by the hands of giants
  For godlike kings of old;
From seagirt Populonia,
  Whose sentinels descry
Sardinia's snowy mountain tops
  Fringing the southern sky;

V

From the proud mart of Pisæ,
  Queen of the western waves,
Where ride Massilia's triremes
  Heavy with fair-haired slaves;

From where sweet Clanis wanders
  Through corn and vines and flowers;
From where Cortona lifts to heaven
  Her diadem of towers.

VI

Tall are the oaks whose acorns
  Drop in dark Auser's rill;
Fat are the stags that champ the boughs
  Of the Ciminian hill;
Beyond all streams Clitumnus
  Is to the herdsman dear;
Best of all pools the fowler loves
  The great Volsinian mere.

VII

But now no stroke of woodman
  Is heard by Auser's rill;
No hunter tracks the stag's green path
  Up the Ciminian hill;
Unwatched along Clitumnus
  Grazes the milk-white steer;
Unharmed the water-fowl may dip
  In the Volsinian mere.

VIII

The harvests of Arretium,
   This year, old men shall reap;
This year, young boys in Umbro 60
   Shall plunge the struggling sheep;
And in the vats of Luna,
   This year, the must shall foam
Round the white feet of laughing girls
   Whose sires have marched to Rome. 65

IX

There be thirty chosen prophets,
   The wisest of the land,
Who alway by Lars Porsena
   Both morn and evening stand:
Evening and morn the Thirty 70
   Have turned the verses o'er,
Traced from the right on linen white°
   By mighty seers of yore.

X

And with one voice the Thirty
   Have their glad answer given: 75
"Go forth, go forth, Lars Porsena;
   Go forth, beloved of Heaven;

Go, and return in glory
  To Clusium's royal dome;
And hang round Nursia's altars
  The golden shields of Rome."

XI

And now hath every city
  Sent up her tale of men;
The foot are fourscore thousand,
  The horse are thousands ten.
Before the gates of Sutrium
  Is met the great array.
A proud man was Lars Porsena
  Upon the trysting day.

XII

For all the Etruscan armies
  Were ranged beneath his eye,
And many a banished Roman,
  And many a stout ally;
And with a mighty following
  To join the muster came
The Tusculan Mamilius,
  Prince of the Latian name.

XIII

But by the yellow Tiber
  Was tumult and affright:
From all the spacious champaign   100
  To Rome men took their flight.
A mile around the city,
  The throng stopped up the ways;
A fearful sight it was to see
  Through two long nights and days.   105

XIV

For aged folks on crutches,
  And women great with child,
And mothers sobbing over babes
  That clung to them and smiled,
And sick men borne in litters   110
  High on the necks of slaves,
And troops of sun-burned husbandmen
  With reaping-hooks and staves,

XV

And droves of mules and asses
  Laden with skins of wine,   115
And endless flocks of goats and sheep,
  And endless herds of kine,

And endless trains of wagons
   That creaked beneath the weight
Of corn-sacks and of household goods,
   Choked every roaring gate.

XVI

Now, from the rock Tarpeian,
   Could the wan burghers spy
The line of blazing villages
   Red in the midnight sky.
The Fathers of the City,
   They sat all night and day,
For every hour some horseman came
   With tidings of dismay.

XVII

To eastward and to westward
   Have spread the Tuscan bands;
Nor house, nor fence, nor dovecote
   In Crustumerium stands.
Verbenna down to Ostia
   Hath wasted all the plain;
Astur hath stormed Janiculum,
   And the stout guards are slain.

XVIII

I wis, in all the Senate,
  There was no heart so bold,
But sore it ached, and fast it beat,   140
  When that ill news was told.
Forthwith up rose the Consul,
  Up rose the Fathers all;
In haste they girded up their gowns,
  And hied them to the wall.   145

XIX

They held a council standing,
  Before the River-Gate;
Short time was there, ye well may guess,
  For musing or debate.
Out spake the Consul roundly: 150
  "The bridge must straight go down;
For, since Janiculum is lost,
  Nought else can save the town."

XX

Just then a scout came flying,
  All wild with haste and fear: 155
"To arms! to arms! Sir Consul:
  Lars Porsena is here."

On the low hills to westward
  The Consul fixed his eye,
And saw the swarthy storm of dust
  Rise fast along the sky.

XXI

And nearer fast and nearer
  Doth the red whirlwind come;
And louder still and still more loud,
From underneath that rolling cloud,
Is heard the trumpet's war-note proud,
  The trampling, and the hum.
And plainly and more plainly
  Now through the gloom appears,
Far to left and far to right,
In broken gleams of dark-blue light,
The long array of helmets bright,
  The long array of spears.

XXII

And plainly and more plainly,
  Above that glimmering line,
Now might ye see the banners
  Of twelve fair cities shine;

But the banner of proud Clusium
   Was highest of them all,
The terror of the Umbrian,
   The terror of the Gaul.

XXIII

And plainly and more plainly
   Now might the burghers know,
By port and vest, by horse and crest,
   Each warlike Lucumo.
There Cilnius of Arretium
   On his fleet roan was seen;
And Astur of the fourfold shield,
Girt with the brand none else may wield,
Tolumnius with the belt of gold,
And dark Verbenna from the hold
   By reedy Thrasymene.

XXIV

Fast by the royal standard,
   O'erlooking all the war,
Lars Porsena of Clusium
   Sat in his ivory car.

By the right wheel rode Mamilius,
   Prince of the Latian name;
And by the left false Sextus,
   That wrought the deed of shame.° 200

XXV

But when the face of Sextus
   Was seen among the foes,
A yell that rent the firmament
   From all the town arose.
On the house-tops was no woman 205
   But spat towards him and hissed,
No child but screamed out curses,
   And shook its little fist.

XXVI

But the Consul's brow was sad,
   And the Consul's speech was low, 210
And darkly looked he at the wall,
   And darkly at the foe.
"Their van will be upon us
   Before the bridge goes down;
And if they once may win the bridge, 215
   What hope to save the town?"

XXVII

Then out spake brave Horatius,
    The Captain of the Gate:
"To every man upon this earth
    Death cometh soon or late.   220
And how can man die better
    Than facing fearful odds,
For the ashes of his fathers,
    And the temples of his Gods,

XXVIII

"And for the tender mother   225
    Who dandled him to rest,
And for the wife who nurses
    His baby at her breast,
And for the holy maidens
    Who feed the eternal flame,   230
To save them from false Sextus
    That wrought the deed of shame?

XXIX

"Hew down the bridge, Sir Consul,
    With all the speed ye may;
I, with two more to help me,   235
    Will hold the foe in play.

In yon strait path a thousand
  May well be stopped by three.
Now who will stand on either hand,
  And keep the bridge with me?"

XXX

Then out spake Spurius Lartius;
  A Ramnian proud was he:
"Lo, I will stand at thy right hand,
  And keep the bridge with thee."
And out spake strong Herminius
  Of Titian blood was he:
"I will abide on thy left side,
  And keep the bridge with thee."

XXXI

"Horatius," quoth the Consul,
  "As thou sayest, so let it be."
And straight against that great array
  Forth went the dauntless Three.
For Romans in Rome's quarrel
  Spared neither land nor gold,
Nor son nor wife, nor limb nor life,
  In the brave days of old.

XXXII

Then none was for a party,
  Then all were for the state;
Then the great men helped the poor,
  And the poor man loved the great: 260
Then lands were fairly portioned;
  Then spoils were fairly sold:
The Romans were like brothers
  In the brave days of old.

XXXIII

Now Roman is to Roman 265
  More hateful than a foe,
And the Tribunes beard the high,
  And the Fathers grind the low.
As we wax hot in faction,
  In battle we wax cold: 270
Wherefore men fight not as they fought
  In the brave days of old.

XXXIV

Now while the Three were tightening
  Their harness on their backs,
The Consul was the foremost man 275
  To take in hand an axe:

And Fathers mixed with Commons
   Seized hatchet, bar, and crow,
And smote upon the planks above,
   And loosed the props below.   280

XXXV

Meanwhile the Tuscan army,
   Right glorious to behold,
Came flashing back the noonday light,
Rank behind rank, like surges bright
   Of a broad sea of gold.   285
Four hundred trumpets sounded
   A peal of warlike glee,
As that great host, with measured tread,
And spears advanced, and ensigns spread,
Rolled slowly towards the bridge's head,   290
   Where stood the dauntless Three.

XXXVI

The Three stood calm and silent,
   And looked upon the foes,
And a great shout of laughter
   From all the vanguard rose;   295

And forth three chiefs came spurring
   Before that deep array;
To earth they sprang, their swords they drew,
And lifted high their shields, and flew
   To win the narrow way;   300

XXXVII

Aunus from green Tifernum,
   Lord of the Hill of Vines;
And Seius, whose eight hundred slaves
   Sicken in Ilva's mines;
And Picus, long to Clusium   305
   Vassal in peace and war,
Who led to fight his Umbrian powers
From that gray crag where, girt with towers,
The fortress of Nequinum lowers
   O'er the pale waves of Nar.   310

XXXVIII

Stout Lartius hurled down Aunus
   Into the stream beneath;
Herminius struck at Seius,
   And clove him to the teeth;

At Picus brave Horatius
   Darted one fiery thrust;
And the proud Umbrian's gilded arms
   Clashed in the bloody dust.

XXXIX

Then Ocnus of Falerii
   Rushed on the Roman Three;
And Lausulus of Urgo,
   The rover of the sea;
And Aruns of Volsinium,
   Who slew the great wild boar,
The great wild boar that had his den
Amidst the reeds of Cosa's fen,
And wasted fields, and slaughtered men,
   Along Albinia's shore.

XL

Herminius smote down Aruns:
   Lartius laid Ocnus low:
Right to the heart of Lausulus
   Horatius sent a blow.
"Lie there," he cried, "fell pirate!
   No more, aghast and pale,

From Ostia's walls the crowd shall mark 335
The track of thy destroying bark.
No more Campania's hinds shall fly
To woods and caverns when they spy
   Thy thrice-accursed sail."

XLI

But now no sound of laughter 340
   Was heard among the foes.
A wild and wrathful clamor
   From all the vanguard rose.
Six spears' length from the entrance
   Halted that deep array, 345
And for a space no man came forth
   To win the narrow way.

XLII

But hark! the cry is Astur:
   And lo! the ranks divide;
And the great Lord of Luna 350
   Comes with his stately stride.
Upon his ample shoulders
   Clangs loud the fourfold shield,
And in his hand he shakes the brand
   Which none but he can wield. 355

XLIII

He smiled on those bold Romans
　A smile serene and high;
He eyed the flinching Tuscans,
　And scorn was in his eye.
Quoth he, "The she-wolf's litter　　　　360
　Stand savagely at bay:
But will ye dare to follow,
　If Astur clears the way?"

XLIV

Then, whirling up his broadsword
　With both hands to the height,　　　　365
He rushed against Horatius,
　And smote with all his might.
With shield and blade Horatius
　Right deftly turned the blow.
The blow, though turned, came yet too nigh;
It missed his helm, but gashed his thigh:　371
The Tuscans raised a joyful cry
　To see the red blood flow.

XLV

He reeled, and on Herminius
　He leaned one breathing-space;　　　　375

Then, like a wild cat mad with wounds,
  Sprang right at Astur's face.
Through teeth, and skull, and helmet
  So fierce a thrust he sped,
The good sword stood a hand-breadth out
  Behind the Tuscan's head. 381

XLVI

And the great Lord of Luna
  Fell at that deadly stroke,
As falls on Mount Alvernus
  A thunder-smitten oak. 385
Far o'er the crashing forest
  The giant arms lie spread;
And the pale augurs, muttering low,
  Gaze on the blasted head.

XLVII

On Astur's throat Horatius 390
  Right firmly pressed his heel;
And thrice and four times tugged amain,
  Ere he wrenched out the steel.
"And see," he cried, "the welcome,
  Fair guests, that waits you here! 395

What noble Lucumo comes next
  To taste our Roman cheer?"

XLVIII

But at his haughty challenge
  A sullen murmur ran,
Mingled of wrath, and shame, and dread,   400
  Along that glittering van.
There lacked not men of prowess,
  Nor men of lordly race;
For all Etruria's noblest
  Were round the fatal place.   405

XLIX

But all Etruria's noblest
  Felt their hearts sink to see
On the earth the bloody corpses,
  In the path the dauntless Three:
And from the ghastly entrance   410
  Where those bold Romans stood,
All shrank, like boys who unaware,
Ranging the woods to start a hare,
Come to the mouth of the dark lair
Where, growling low, a fierce old bear   415
  Lies amidst bones and blood.

L

Was none who would be foremost
　To lead such dire attack;
But those behind cried, "Forward!"
　And those before cried, "Back!"　　　420
And backward now and forward
　Wavers the deep array;
And on the tossing sea of steel
To and fro the standards reel;
And the victorious trumpet-peal　　　425
　Dies fitfully away.

LI

Yet one man for one moment
　Stood out before the crowd;
Well known was he to all the Three,
　And they gave him greeting loud.　　　430
"Now welcome, welcome, Sextus!
　Now welcome to thy home!
Why dost thou stay, and turn away?
　Here lies the road to Rome."

LII

Thrice looked he at the city;　　　435
　Thrice looked he at the dead;

And thrice came on in fury,
  And thrice turned back in dread:
And, white with fear and hatred,
  Scowled at the narrow way   440
Where, wallowing in a pool of blood,
  The bravest Tuscans lay.

LIII

But meanwhile axe and lever
  Have manfully been plied;
And now the bridge hangs tottering   445
  Above the boiling tide.
"Come back, come back, Horatius!"
  Loud cried the Fathers all.
"Back, Lartius! back, Herminius!
  Back, ere the ruin fall!"   450

LIV

Back darted Spurius Lartius;
  Herminius darted back:
And, as they passed, beneath their feet
  They felt the timbers crack.
But when they turned their faces,   455
  And on the farther shore

LV

But with a crash like thunder
  Fell every loosened beam, 460
And, like a dam, the mighty wreck
  Lay right athwart the stream;
And a long shout of triumph
  Rose from the walls of Rome,
As to the highest turret-tops 465
  Was splashed the yellow foam.

LVI

And like a horse unbroken
  When first he feels the rein,
The furious river struggled hard,
  And tossed his tawny mane, 470
And burst the curb, and bounded,
  Rejoicing to be free,
And whirling down, in fierce career,
Battlement, and plank, and pier,
  Rushed headlong to the sea. 475

LVII

Alone stood brave Horatius,
   But constant still in mind;
Thrice thirty thousand foes before,
   And the broad flood behind.
"Down with him!" cried false Sextus,   480
   With a smile on his pale face.
"Now yield thee," cried Lars Porsena,
   "Now yield thee to our grace."

LVIII

Round turned he, as not deigning
   Those craven ranks to see;   485
Nought spake he to Lars Porsena,
   To Sextus nought spake he;
But he saw on Palatinus
   The white porch of his home;
And he spake to the noble river   490
   That rolls by the towers of Rome.

LIX

"Oh, Tiber! father Tiber!
   To whom the Romans pray,

A Roman's life, a Roman's arms,
  Take thou in charge this day."
So he spake, and speaking sheathed
  The good sword by his side,
And with his harness on his back,
  Plunged headlong in the tide.

LX

No sound of joy or sorrow
  Was heard from either bank;
But friends and foes, in dumb surprise,
With parted lips and straining eyes,
  Stood gazing where he sank;
And when above the surges
  They saw his crest appear,
All Rome sent forth a rapturous cry,
And even the ranks of Tuscany
  Could scarce forbear to cheer.

LXI

But fiercely ran the current,
  Swollen high by months of rain:
And fast his blood was flowing,
  And he was sore in pain,

And heavy with his armor,
  And spent with changing blows:
And oft they thought him sinking,
  But still again he rose.

LXII

Never, I ween, did swimmer,
  In such an evil case,
Struggle through such a raging flood
  Safe to the landing-place:
But his limbs were borne up bravely
  By the brave heart within,
And our good father Tiber
  Bore bravely up his chin.[1]

LXIII

" Curse on him!" quoth false Sextus;
  " Will not the villain drown?

---

[1] " Our ladye bare upp her chinne."
  " Ballad of Childe Waters."

" Never heavier man and horse
  Stemmed a midnight torrent's force;
    *   *   *   *
  Yet, through good heart and our Lady's grace,
  At length he gained the landing-place."
  " Lay of the last Minstrel," I.

But for this stay, ere close of day
　　We should have sacked the town!"
"Heaven help him!" quoth Lars Porsena, 530
　　" And bring him safe to shore;
For such a gallant feat of arms
　　Was never seen before."

LXIV

And now he feels the bottom;
　　Now on dry earth he stands; 535
Now round him throng the Fathers
　　To press his gory hands;
And now, with shouts and clapping,
　　And noise of weeping loud,
He enters through the River-Gate, 540
　　Borne by the joyous crowd.

LXV

They gave him of the corn-land,
　　That was of public right,
As much as two strong oxen
　　Could plough from morn till night; 545
And they made a molten image,
　　And set it up on high,

LXVI

It stands in the Comitium,° 550
  Plain for all folk to see;
Horatius in his harness,
  Halting upon one knee:
And underneath is written,
  In letters all of gold, 555
How valiantly he kept the bridge,
  In the brave days of old.

LXVII

And still his name sounds stirring
  Unto the men of Rome,
As the trumpet-blast that cries to them 560
  To charge the Volscian home;
And wives still pray to Juno
  For boys with hearts as bold
As his who kept the bridge so well.
  In the brave days of old. 565

LXVIII

And in the nights of winter,
  When the cold north winds blow,

And the long howling of the wolves
  Is heard amidst the snow;
When round the lonely cottage   570
  Roars loud the tempest's din,
And the good logs of Algidus
  Roar louder yet within;

LXIX

When the oldest cask is opened,
  And the largest lamp is lit;   575
When the chestnuts glow in the embers,
  And the kid turns on the spit;
When young and old in circle
  Around the firebrands close;
When the girls are weaving baskets,   580
  And the lads are shaping bows;

LXX

When the goodman mends his armor,
  And trims his helmet's plume;
When the goodwife's shuttle merrily
  Goes flashing through the loom: 585

With weeping and with laughter
　Still is the story told,
How well Horatius kept the bridge
　In the brave days of old.

THE BATTLE OF THE LAKE REGILLUS

A LAY SUNG AT THE FEAST OF CASTOR AND POLLUX ON
THE IDES OF QUINTILIS IN THE YEAR OF THE CITY
CCCCLI

I

Ho, trumpets, sound a war-note!
  Ho, lictors,° clear the way!
The Knights will ride, in all their pride,
  Along the streets to-day.
To-day the doors and windows
  Are hung with garlands all,
From Castor in the Forum,
  To Mars without the wall.
Each Knight is robed in purple,
  With olive each is crowned;
A gallant war-horse under each
  Paws haughtily the ground.
While flows the Yellow River,°
  While stands the Sacred Hill,°

The proud Ides of Quintilis° 15
  Shall have such honor still.
Gay are the Martian Kalends,
  December's Nones are gay,
But the proud Ides, when the squadron rides,
  Shall be Rome's whitest day. 20

II

Unto the Great Twin Brethren
  We keep this solemn feast.
Swift, swift, the Great Twin Brethren
  Came spurring from the east.
They came o'er wild Parthenius 25
  Tossing in waves of pine,
O'er Cirrha's dome, o'er Adria's foam,
  O'er purple Apennine,
From where with flutes and dances
  Their ancient mansion rings, 30
In lordly Lacedæmon,
  The City of two kings,
To where, by Lake Regillus,
  Under the Porcian height,
All in the lands of Tusculum, 35
  Was fought the glorious fight.

III

Now on the place of slaughter
   Are cots and sheepfolds seen,
And rows of vines, and fields of wheat,
   And apple orchards green;
The swine crush the big acorns
   That fall from Corne's oaks.
Upon the turf by the Fair Fount
   The reaper's pottage smokes.
The fisher baits his angle;
   The hunter twangs his bow;
Little they think on those strong limbs
   That moulder deep below.
Little they think how sternly
   That day the trumpets pealed;
How in the slippery swamp of blood
   Warrior and war-horse reeled;
How wolves came with fierce gallop,
   And crows on eager wings,
To tear the flesh of captains,
   And peck the eyes of kings;
How thick the dead lay scattered
   Under the Porcian height;

How through the gates of Tusculum
  Raved the wild stream of flight; 60
And how the Lake Regillus
  Bubbled with crimson foam,
What time the Thirty Cities°
  Came forth to war with Rome.

IV

But, Roman, when thou standest 65
  Upon that holy ground,
Look thou with heed on the dark rock
  That girds the dark lake round.
So shalt thou see a hoof-mark
  Stamped deep into the flint: 70
It was no hoof of mortal steed
  That made so strange a dint:
There to the Great Twin Brethren
  Vow thou thy vows, and pray
That they, in tempest and in fight, 75
  Will keep thy head alway.

V

Since last the Great Twin Brethren
  Of mortal eyes were seen,

Have years gone by an hundred
    And fourscore and thirteen. 80
That summer a Virginius
    Was consul first in place;
The second was stout Aulus,
    Of the Posthumian race.
The Herald of the Latines 85
    From Gabii came in state:
The Herald of the Latines
    Passed through Rome's Eastern Gate:
The Herald of the Latines
    Did in our Forum stand; 90
And there he did his office,°
    A sceptre in his hand.

VI

"Hear, Senators and people
    Of the good town of Rome,
The Thirty Cities charge you 95
    To bring the Tarquins home;
And if ye still be stubborn
    To work the Tarquins wrong,
The Thirty Cities warn you,
    Look that your walls be strong." 100

VII

Then spake the Consul Aulus,
  He spake a bitter jest:
"Once the jays sent a message
  Unto the eagle's nest: —
Now yield thou up thine eyrie   105
  Unto the carrion-kite,
Or come forth valiantly, and face
  The jays in deadly fight. —
Forth looked in wrath the eagle;
  And carrion-kite and jay,   110
Soon as they saw his beak and claw,
  Fled screaming far away."

VIII

The Herald of the Latines
  Hath hied him back in state:
The Fathers of the City   115
  Are met in high debate.
Then spake the elder Consul,
  An ancient man and wise:
"Now hearken, Conscript Fathers,
  To that which I advise.   120

In seasons of great peril
  'Tis good that one bear sway;
Then choose we a Dictator,
  Whom all men shall obey.
Camerium knows how deeply   125
  The sword of Aulus bites,
And all our city calls him
  The man of seventy fights.
Then let him be Dictator
  For six months and no more,   130
And have a Master of the Knights,
  And axes twenty-four."

IX

So Aulus was Dictator,
  The man of seventy fights;
He made Æbutius Elva   135
  His Master of the Knights.
On the third morn thereafter,
  At dawning of the day,
Did Aulus and Æbutius
  Set forth with their array.   140
Sempronius Atratinus
  Was left in charge at home,

With boys, and with gray-headed men,
   To keep the walls of Rome.
Hard by the Lake Regillus   145
   Our camp was pitched at night:
Eastward a mile the Latines lay,
   Under the Porcian height.
Far over hill and valley
   Their mighty host was spread;   150
And with their thousand watch-fires
   The midnight sky was red.

X

Up rose the golden morning
   Over the Porcian height,
The proud Ides of Quintilis   155
   Marked evermore with white.
Not without secret trouble
   Our bravest saw the foes;
For girt by threescore thousand spears
   The thirty standards rose.   160
From every warlike city
   That boasts the Latian name,
Foredoomed to dogs and vultures,
   That gallant army came;

From Setia's purple vineyards,   165
  From Norba's ancient wall,
From the white streets of Tusculum,
  The proudest town of all;
From where the Witch's Fortress
  O'erhangs the dark-blue seas;   170
From the still glassy lake that sleeps
  Beneath Aricia's trees —
Those trees in whose dim shadow
  The ghastly priest° doth reign,
The priest who slew the slayer,   175
  And shall himself be slain;
From the drear banks of Ufens,
  Where flights of marsh-fowl play,
And buffaloes lie wallowing
  Through the hot summer's day;   180
From the gigantic watch-towers,
  No work of earthly men,
Whence Cora's sentinels o'erlook
  The never-ending fen;
From the Laurentian jungle,   185
  The wild hog's reedy home;
From the green steeps whence Anio leaps
  In floods of snow-white foam.

XI

Aricia, Cora, Norba,
   Velitræ, with the might
Of Setia and of Tusculum,
   Were marshalled on the right:
The leader was Mamilius,
   Prince of the Latian name;
Upon his head a helmet
   Of red gold shone like flame;
High on a gallant charger
   Of dark-gray hue he rode;
Over his gilded armor
   A vest of purple flowed,
Woven in the land of sunrise
   By Syria's dark-browed daughters,
And by the sails of Carthage brought
   Far o'er the southern waters.

XII

Lavinium and Laurentum
   Had on the left their post,
With all the banners of the marsh
   And banners of the coast.

Their leader was false Sextus,
   That wrought the deed of shame: 210
With restless pace and haggard face
   To his last field he came.
Men said he saw strange visions
   Which none beside might see,
And that strange sounds were in his ears 215
   Which none might hear but he.
A woman fair° and stately,
   But pale as are the dead,
Oft through the watches of the night
   Sat spinning by his bed. 220
And as she plied the distaff,
   In a sweet voice and low
She sang of great old houses,
   And fights fought long ago.
So spun she, and so sang she, 225
   Until the east was gray.
Then pointed to her bleeding breast,
   And shrieked, and fled away.

XIII

But in the centre thickest
   Were ranged the shields of foes, 230

And from the centre loudest
   The cry of battle rose.
There Tibur marched and Pedum
   Beneath proud Tarquin's rule,
And Ferentinum of the rock,   235
   And Gabii of the pool.
There rode the Volscian succors:
   There, in a dark stern ring,
The Roman exiles gathered close
   Around the ancient king.   240
Though white as Mount Soracte,
   When winter nights are long,
His beard flowed down o'er mail and belt,
   His heart and hand were strong:
Under his hoary eyebrows   245
   Still flashed forth quenchless rage:
And, if the lance shook in his gripe,
   'Twas more with hate than age.
Close at his side was Titus
   On an Apulian steed,   250
Titus, the youngest Tarquin,
   Too good for such a breed.

XIV

Now on each side the leaders
　Give signal for the charge;
And on each side the footmen　　　　255
　Strode on with lance and targe;
And on each side the horsemen
　Struck their spurs deep in gore,
And front to front the armies
　Met with a mighty roar:　　　　260
And under that great battle
　The earth with blood was red;
And, like the Pomptine fog at morn,
　The dust hung overhead;
And louder still and louder　　　　265
　Rose from the darkened field
The braying of the war-horns,
　The clang of sword and shield,
The rush of squadrons sweeping
　Like whirlwinds o'er the plain,　　　　270
The shouting of the slayers,
　And screeching of the slain.

XV

False Sextus rode out foremost,
　His look was high and bold;

His corslet was of bison's hide, 275
    Plated with steel and gold.
As glares the famished eagle
    From the Digentian rock
On a choice lamb that bounds alone
    Before Bandusia's flock, 280
Herminius glared on Sextus,
    And came with eagle speed,
Herminius on black Auster,
    Brave champion on brave steed;
In his right hand the broadsword 285
    That kept the bridge so well,
And on his helm the crown he won
    When proud Fidenæ fell.
Woe to the maid whose lover
    Shall cross his path to-day! 290
False Sextus saw, and trembled,
    And turned and fled away.
As turns, as flies the woodman
    In the Calabrian brake,
When through the reeds gleams the round eye
    Of that fell speckled snake; 296
So turned, so fled, false Sextus,
    And hid him in the rear,

XVI

But far to north Æbutius,
   The Master of the Knights,
Gave Tubero of Norba
   To feed the Porcian kites.
Next under those red horse-hoofs
   Flaccus of Setia lay;
Better had he been pruning
   Among his elms that day.
Mamilius saw the slaughter,
   And tossed his golden crest,
And towards the Master of the Knights
   Through the thick battle pressed.
Æbutius smote Mamilius
   So fiercely on the shield
That the great lord of Tusculum
   Well nigh rolled on the field.
Mamilius smote Æbutius,
   With a good aim and true,
Just where the neck and shoulder join,
   And pierced him through and through;

And brave Æbutius Elva
  Fell swooning to the ground:
But a thick wall of bucklers
  Encompassed him around.
His clients from the battle   325
  Bare him some little space,
And filled a helm from the dark lake,
  And bathed his brow and face;
And when at last he opened
  His swimming eyes to light,   330
Men say, the earliest word he spake
  Was, "Friends, how goes the fight?"

XVII

But meanwhile in the centre
  Great deeds of arms were wrought;
There Aulus the Dictator   335
  And there Valerius fought.
Aulus with his good broadsword
  A bloody passage cleared
To where, amidst the thickest foes,
  He saw the long white beard.   340
Flat lighted that good broadsword
  Upon proud Tarquin's head.

He dropped the lance: he dropped the reins:
   He fell as fall the dead.
Down Aulus springs to slay him,   345
   With eyes like coals of fire;
But faster Titus hath sprung down,
   And hath bestrode his sire.
Latian captains, Roman knights,
   Fast down to earth they spring,   350
And hand to hand they fight on foot
   Around the ancient king.
First Titus gave tall Cæso
   A death-wound in the face;
Tall Cæso was the bravest man   355
   Of the brave Fabian race:
Aulus slew Rex of Gabii,
   The priest of Juno's shrine;
Valerius smote down Julius,
   Of Rome's great Julian line;   360
Julius, who left his mansion
   High on the Velian hill,
And through all turns of weal and woe
   Followed proud Tarquin still.
Now right across proud Tarquin   365
   A corpse was Julius laid;

And Titus groaned with rage and grief,
   And at Valerius made.
Valerius struck at Titus,
   And lopped off half his crest; 370
But Titus stabbed Valerius
   A span deep in the breast.
Like a mast snapped by the tempest,
   Valerius reeled and fell.
Ah! woe is me for the good house 375
   That loves the people well!
Then shouted loud the Latines;
   And with one rush they bore
The struggling Romans backward
   Three lances' length and more: 380
And up they took proud Tarquin,
   And laid him on a shield,
And four strong yeomen bare him,
   Still senseless, from the field.

XVIII

But fiercer grew the fighting 385
   Around Valerius dead;
For Titus dragged him by the foot,
   And Aulus by the head.

"On, Latines, on!" quoth Titus,
  "See how the rebels fly!"
"Romans, stand firm!" quoth Aulus,
  "And win this fight, or die!
They must not give Valerius
  To raven and to kite;
For aye Valerius loathed the wrong,
  And aye upheld the right;
And for your wives and babies
  In the front rank he fell.
Now play the men for the good house
  That loves the people well!"

XIX

Then tenfold round the body
  The roar of battle rose,
Like the roar of a burning forest,
  When a strong north wind blows.
Now backward, and now forward,
  Rocked furiously the fray,
Till none could see Valerius,
  And none wist where he lay.
For shivered arms and ensigns
  Were heaped there in a mound,

And corpses stiff, and dying men
  That writhed and gnawed the ground;
And wounded horses kicking,
  And snorting purple foam:
Right well did such a couch befit   415
  A Consular of Rome.

XX

But north looked the Dictator;
  North looked he long and hard;
And spake to Caius Cossus,
  The Captain of his Guard;   420
"Caius, of all the Romans
  Thou hast the keenest sight;
Say, what through yonder storm of dust
  Comes from the Latian right?"

XXI

Then answered Caius Cossus,   425
  "I see an evil sight;
The banner of proud Tusculum
  Comes from the Latian right;
I see the pluméd horsemen;
  And far before the rest   430

I see the dark-gray charger,
  I see the purple vest;
I see the golden helmet
  That shines far off like flame;
So ever rides Mamilius,   435
  Prince of the Latian name."

XXII

"Now hearken, Caius Cossus:
  Spring on thy horse's back;
Ride as the wolves of Apennine
  Were all upon thy track;   440
Haste to our southward battle:
  And never draw thy rein
Until thou find Herminius,
  And bid him come amain."

XXIII

So Aulus spake, and turned him   445
  Again to that fierce strife;
And Caius Cossus mounted,
  And rode for death and life.
Loud clanged beneath his horse-hoofs
  The helmets of the dead,   450

And many a curdling pool of blood
   Splashed him from heel to head.
So came he far to southward,
   Where fought the Roman host,
Against the banners of the marsh
   And banners of the coast.
Like corn before the sickle
   The stout Lavinians fell,
Beneath the edge of the true sword
   That kept the bridge so well.

XXIV

"Herminius! Aulus greets thee;
   He bids thee come with speed,
To help our central battle,
   For sore is there our need;
There was the youngest Tarquin,
   And there the Crest of Flame,
The Tusculan Mamilius,
   Prince of the Latian name.
Valerius hath fallen fighting
   In front of our array:
And Aulus of the seventy fields
   Alone upholds the day."

XXV

Herminius beat his bosom.
  But never a word he spake.
He clasped his hand on Auster's mane: 475
  He gave the reins a shake.
Away, away, went Auster,
  Like an arrow from the bow:
Black Auster was the fleetest steed
  From Aufidus to Po. 480

XXVI

Right glad were all the Romans
  Who, in that hour of dread,
Against great odds bare up the war
  Around Valerius dead,
When from the south the cheering 485
  Rose with a mighty swell;
" Herminius comes, Herminius,
  Who kept the bridge so well ! "

XXVII

Mamilius spied Herminius,
  And dashed across the way. 490

"Herminius! I have sought thee
  Through many a bloody day.
One of us two, Herminius,
  Shall never more go home.
I will lay on for Tusculum   495
  And lay thou on for Rome!"

XXVIII

All round them paused the battle
  While met in mortal fray,
The Roman and the Tusculan,
  The horses black and gray.   500
Herminius smote Mamilius
  Through breast-plate and through breast;
And fast flowed out the purple blood
  Over the purple vest.
Mamilius smote Herminius   505
  Through head-piece and through head,
And side by side those chiefs of pride
  Together fell down dead.
Down fell they dead together
  In a great lake of gore;   510
And still stood all who saw them fall
  While men might count a score.

XXIX

Fast, fast, with heels wild spurning,
    The dark-gray charger fled:
He burst through ranks of fighting men,
    He sprang o'er heaps of dead.
His bridle far out-streaming,
    His flanks all blood and foam,
He sought the southern mountains,
    The mountains of his home.
The pass was steep and rugged,
    The wolves they howled and whined;
But he ran like a whirlwind up the pass,
    And he left the wolves behind.
Through many a startled hamlet
    Thundered his flying feet;
He rushed through the gate of Tusculum,
    He rushed up the long white street,
He rushed by tower and temple,
    And paused not from his race
Till he stood before his master's door
    In the stately market-place.
And straightway round him gathered
    A pale and trembling crowd,

LAYS OF ANCIENT ROME

And when they knew him, cries of rage 535
   Brake forth, and wailing loud:
And women rent their tresses
   For their great prince's fall;
And old men girt on their old swords,
   And went to man the wall. 540

XXX

But, like a graven image,
   Black Auster kept his place,
And ever wistfully he looked
   Into his master's face.
The raven-mane that daily, 545
   With pats and fond caresses,
The young Herminia washed and combed,
   And twined in even tresses,
And decked with colored ribands
   From her own gay attire, 550
Hung sadly o'er her father's corpse
   In carnage and in mire.
Forth with a shout sprang Titus,
   And seized black Auster's rein.
Then Aulus sware a fearful oath, 555
   And ran at him amain.

"The furies of thy brother
  With me and mine abide,
If one of your accursed house
  Upon black Auster ride!"   560
As on an Alpine watch-tower
  From heaven comes down the flame,
Full on the neck of Titus
  The blade of Aulus came:
And out the red blood spouted,   565
  In a wide arch and tall,
As spouts a fountain in the court
  Of some rich Capuan's hall.
The knees of all the Latines
  Were loosened with dismay,   570
When dead, on dead Herminius,
  The bravest Tarquin lay.

XXXI

And Aulus the Dictator
  Stroked Auster's raven mane,
With heed he looked unto the girths, 575
  With heed unto the rein.
"Now bear me well, black Auster,
  Into yon thick array:

And thou and I will have revenge
   For thy good lord this day."

XXXII

So spake he; and was buckling
   Tighter black Auster's band,
When he was aware of a princely pair
   That rode at his right hand.
So like they were, no mortal
   Might one from other know:
White as snow their armor was;
   Their steeds were white as snow.
Never on earthly anvil
   Did such rare armor gleam;
And never did such gallant steeds
   Drink of an earthly stream.

XXXIII

And all who saw them trembled,
   And pale grew every cheek;
And Aulus the Dictator
   Scarce gathered voice to speak.
"Say by what name men call you?
   What city is your home?

And wherefore ride ye in such guise
  Before the ranks of Rome?"

XXXIV

"By many names men call us;
  In many lands we dwell:
Well Samothracia knows us;
  Cyrene knows us well.
Our house in gay Tarentum
  Is hung each morn with flowers:
High o'er the masts of Syracuse
  Our marble portal towers;
But by the proud Eurotas
  Is our dear native home;
And for the right we come to fight
  Before the ranks of Rome."

XXXV

So answered those strange horsemen,
  And each couched low his spear;
And forthwith all the ranks of Rome
  Were bold, and of good cheer:
And on the thirty armies
  Came wonder and affright,

And Ardea wavered on the left,
  And Cora on the right.
"Rome to the charge!" cried Aulus;
  "The foe begins to yield!
Charge for the hearth of Vesta!°
  Charge for the Golden Shield!
Let no man stop to plunder,
  But slay, and slay, and slay;
The gods who live forever
  Are on our side to-day."

XXXVI

Then the fierce trumpet-flourish
  From earth to heaven arose;
The kites know well the long stern swell
  That bids the Romans close.
Then the good sword of Aulus
  Was lifted up to slay;
Then, like a crag down Apennine,
  Rushed Auster through the fray.
But under those strange horsemen
  Still thicker lay the slain;
And after those strange horses
  Black Auster toiled in vain.

Behind them Rome's long battle
  Came rolling on the foe,
Ensigns dancing wild above,
  Blades all in line below.
So comes the Po in flood-time   645
  Upon the Celtic plain:
So comes the squall, blacker than night,
  Upon the Adrian main.
Now by our sire Quirinus,
  It was a goodly sight   650
To see the thirty standards
  Swept down the tide of flight.
So flies the spray of Adria
  When the black squall doth blow,
So corn-sheaves in the flood-time   655
  Spin down the whirling Po.
False Sextus to the mountains
  Turned first his horse's head;
And fast fled Ferentinum,
  And fast Lanuvium fled.   660
The horsemen of Nomentum
  Spurred hard out of the fray;
The footmen of Velitræ
  Threw shield and spear away.

And underfoot was trampled, 665
　　Amidst the mud and gore,
The banner of proud Tusculum,
　　That never stooped before:
And down went Flavius Faustus,
　　Who led his stately ranks 670
From where the apple blossoms wave
　　On Anio's echoing banks,
And Tullus of Arpinum,
　　Chief of the Volscian aids,
And Metius with the long fair curls, 675
　　The love of Anxur's maids,
And the white head of Vulso,
　　The great Arician seer,
And Nepos of Laurentum,
　　The hunter of the deer; 680
And in the back false Sextus
　　Felt the good Roman steel,
And wriggling in the dust he died,
　　Like a worm beneath the wheel:
And fliers and pursuers 685
　　Were mingled in a mass;
And far away the battle
　　Went roaring through the pass.

XXXVII

Sempronius Atratinus
   Sat in the Eastern Gate,   690
Beside him were three Fathers,
   Each in his chair of state;
Fabius, whose nine stout grandsons
   That day were in the field,
And Manlius, eldest of the Twelve   695
   Who keep the Golden Shield;
And Sergius, the High Pontiff,
   For wisdom far renowned;
In all Etruria's colleges
   Was no such Pontiff found.   700
And all around the portal,
   And high above the wall,
Stood a great throng of people,
   But sad and silent all;
Young lads, and stooping elders   705
   That might not bear the mail,
Matrons with lips that quivered,
   And maids with faces pale.
Since the first gleam of daylight,
   Sempronius had not ceased   710

To listen for the rushing
   Of horse-hoofs from the east.
The mist of eve was rising,
   The sun was hastening down,
When he was aware of a princely pair   715
   Fast pricking towards the town.
So like they were, man never
   Saw twins so like before;
Red with gore their armor was,
   Their steeds were red with gore.   720

XXXVIII

" Hail to the great Asylum!
   Hail to the hill-tops seven!
Hail to the fire that burns for aye,
   And the shield that fell from heaven!
This day, by Lake Regillus,   725
   Under the Porcian height,
All in the lands of Tusculum
   Was fought a glorious fight.
To-morrow your Dictator
   Shall bring in triumph home   730
The spoils of thirty cities
   To deck the shrines of Rome! "

XXXIX

Then burst from that great concourse
  A shout that shook the towers,
And some ran north, and some ran south, 735
  Crying, " The day is ours! "
But on rode these strange horsemen,
  With slow and lordly pace;
And none who saw their bearing
  Durst ask their name or race. 740
On rode they to the Forum,
  While laurel-boughs and flowers,
From house-tops and from windows,
  Fell on their crests in showers.
When they drew nigh to Vesta, 745
  They vaulted down amain,
And washed their horses in the well
  That springs by Vesta's fane.
And straight again they mounted,
  And rode to Vesta's door; 750
Then, like a blast, away they passed,
  And no man saw them more.

XL

And all the people trembled,
  And pale grew every cheek;

And Sergius the High Pontiff 755
   Alone found voice to speak:
"The gods who live for ever
   Have fought for Rome to-day!
These be the Great Twin Brethren
   To whom the Dorians pray. 760
Back comes the Chief in triumph,
   Who, in the hour of fight,
Hath seen the Great Twin Brethren
   In harness on his right.
Safe comes the ship to haven, 765
   Through billows and through gales,
If once the Great Twin Brethren
   Sit shining on the sails.
Wherefore they washed their horses
   In Vesta's holy well, 770
Wherefore they rode to Vesta's door,
   I know, but may not tell.
Here, hard by Vesta's Temple,
   Build we a stately dome
Unto the Great Twin Brethren 775
   Who fought so well for Rome.
And when the months returning
   Bring back this day of fight,

The proud Ides of Quintilis,
  Marked evermore with white,   780
Unto the Great Twin Brethren
  Let all the people throng,
With chaplets and with offerings,
  With music and with song;
And let the doors and windows   785
  Be hung with garlands all,
And let the Knights be summoned
  To Mars without the wall:
Thence let them ride in purple
  With joyous trumpet-sound,   790
Each mounted on his war-horse,
  And each with olive crowned;
And pass in solemn order
  Before the sacred dome,
Where dwell the Great Twin Brethren   795
  Who fought so well for Rome!"

VIRGINIA

FRAGMENTS OF A LAY SUNG IN THE FORUM ON THE DAY WHEREON LUCIUS SEXTIUS SEXTINUS LATERANUS AND CAIUS LICINIUS CALVUS STOLO WERE ELECTED TRIBUNES OF THE COMMONS THE FIFTH TIME, IN THE YEAR OF THE CITY CCCLXXXII

Ye good men of the Commons, with loving hearts and true,
Who stand by the bold Tribunes that still have stood by you,
Come, make a circle round me, and mark my tale with care,
A tale of what Rome once hath borne, of what Rome yet may bear.
This is no Grecian fable, of fountains running wine, 5
Of maids° with snaky tresses, or sailors turned to swine.
Here, in this very Forum, under the noonday sun,
In sight of all the people, the bloody deed was done.
Old men still creep among us who saw that fearful day,
Just seventy years and seven ago, when the wicked Ten° bare sway. 10

Of all the wicked Ten still the names are held accursed,
And of all the wicked Ten Appius Claudius was the worst.
He stalked along the Forum like King Tarquin in his pride:
Twelve axes waited on him, six marching on a side;
The townsmen shrank to right and left, and eyed askance with fear 15
His lowering brow, his curling mouth which always seemed to sneer:
That brow of hate, that mouth of scorn, marks all the kindred still;
For never was there Claudius yet but wished the Commons ill;
Nor lacks he fit attendance; for, close behind his heels,
With outstretched chin and crouching pace, the client° Marcus steals, 20
His loins girt up to run with speed, be the errand what it may,
And the smile flickering on his cheek, for aught his lord may say.
Such varlets pimp and jest for hire among the lying Greeks:
Such varlets still are paid to hoot when brave Licinius speaks.

Where'er ye shed the honey, the buzzing flies will crowd;
Where'er ye fling the carrion, the raven's croak is loud;
Where'er down Tiber garbage floats, the greedy pike ye see;
And wheresoe'er such lord is found, such client still will be.
Just then, as through one cloudless chink in a black stormy sky
Shines out the dewy morning-star, a fair young girl came by.
With her small tablets in her hand, and her satchel on her arm,
Home she went bounding from the school, nor dreamed of shame or harm;
And past those dreaded axes she innocently ran,
With bright, frank brow that had not learned to blush at gaze of man;
And up the Sacred Street° she turned, and, as she danced along,
She warbled gayly to herself lines of the good old song,
How for a sport the princes came spurring from the camp,
And found Lucrece, combing the fleece, under the midnight lamp.

The maiden sang as sings the lark, when up he darts his flight,
From his nest in the green April corn, to meet the morning light; 40
And Appius heard her sweet young voice, and saw her sweet young face,
And loved her with the accursed love of his accursed race,
And all along the Forum, and up the Sacred Street,
His vulture eye pursued the trip of those small glancing feet.

Over the Alban mountains the light of morning broke; 45
From all the roofs of the Seven Hills° curled the thin wreaths of smoke:
The city-gates were opened; the Forum all alive,
With buyers and with sellers, was humming like a hive:
Blithely on brass and timber the craftsman's stroke was ringing,
And blithely o'er her panniers the market girl was singing, 50
And blithely young Virginia came smiling from her home;

Ah! woe for young Virginia, the sweetest maid in Rome!
With her small tablets in her hand, and her satchel on her arm,
Forth she went bounding to the school, nor dreamed of shame or harm.
She crossed the Forum shining with stalls in alleys gay 55
And just had reached the very spot whereon I stand this day,
When up the varlet Marcus came; not such as when erewhile
He crouched behind his patron's heels with the true client smile:
He came with lowering forehead, swollen features and clenched fist,
And strode across Virginia's path, and caught her by the wrist. 60
Hard strove the frightened maiden, and screamed with look aghast;
And at her scream from right and left the folk came running fast.
The money-changer Crispus, with his thin silver hairs,
And Hanno from the stately booth glittering with Punic wares,

And the strong smith Muræna, grasping a half-forged
    brand, 65
And Volero the flesher, his cleaver in his hand.
All came in wrath and wonder; for all knew that fair
    child,
And, as she passed them twice a day, all kissed their
    hands and smiled;
And the strong smith Muræna gave Marcus such a blow,
The Caitiff reeled three paces back, and let the maiden
    go. 70
Yet glared he fiercely round him, and growled in harsh,
    fell tone,
" She's mine, and I will have her: I seek but for mine
    own:
She is my slave, born in my house, and stolen away and
    sold,
The year of the sore sickness, ere she was twelve hours
    old.
'Twas in the sad September, the month of wail and
    fright, 75
Two augurs were borne forth that morn; the Consul died
    ere night.
I wait on Appius Claudius, I waited on his sire:
Let him who works the client wrong beware the patron's
    ire!"

So spake the varlet Marcus; and dread and silence came
On all the people at the sound of the great Claudian name. 80
For then there was no Tribune to speak the word of might,
Which makes the rich man tremble, and guards the poor man's right.
There was no brave Licinius, no honest Sextius then;
But all the city, in great fear, obeyed the wicked Ten.
Yet ere the varlet Marcus again might seize the maid, 85
Who clung tight to Muræna's skirt, and sobbed and shrieked for aid,
Forth through the throng of gazers the young Icilius pressed,
And stamped his foot, and rent his gown, and smote upon his breast,
And sprang upon that column, by many a minstrel sung,
Whereon three mouldering helmets, three rusting swords are hung, 90
And beckoned to the people, and in bold voice and clear
Poured thick and fast the burning words which tyrants quake to hear.

"Now, by your children's cradles, now by your fathers' graves,
Be men to-day, Quirites, or be for ever slaves!
For this did Servius give us laws? For this did Lucrece bleed?
For this was the great vengeance wrought on Tarquin's evil seed?
For this did those false sons make red the axes of their sire?
For this did Scævola's° right hand hiss in the Tuscan fire?
Shall the vile fox-earth awe the race that stormed the lion's den?
Shall we, who could not brook one lord, crouch to the wicked Ten?
Oh, for that ancient spirit which curbed the Senate's will!
Oh, for the tents which in old time whitened the Sacred Hill!
In those brave days our fathers stood firmly side by side;
They faced the Marcian fury; they tamed the Fabian pride:
They drove the fiercest Quinctius an outcast forth from Rome;

And upon Appius Claudius great fear and trembling came, 245
For never was a Claudius yet brave against aught but shame.
Though the great houses love us not, we own, to do them right,
That the great houses, all save one, have borne them well in fight.
Still Caius of Corioli,° his triumphs and his wrongs,
His vengeance and his mercy, live in our camp-fire songs. 250
Beneath the yoke of Furius oft have Gaul and Tuscan bowed;
And Rome may bear the pride of him of whom herself is proud.
But evermore a Claudius shrinks from a stricken field,
And changes color like a maid at sight of sword and shield.
The Claudian triumphs all were won within the city towers; 255
The Claudian yoke was never pressed on any necks but ours.
A Cossus, like a wild-cat, springs ever at the face;
A Fabius rushed like a boar against the shouting chase;

But the vile Claudian litter, raging with currish spite,
Still yelps and snaps at those who run, still runs from those who smite. 260
So now 'twas seen of Appius. When stones began to fly,
He shook, and crouched, and wrung his hands, and smote upon his thigh.
"Kind clients, honest lictors, stand by me in this fray!
Must I be torn in pieces? Home, home, the nearest way!"
While yet he spake, and looked around with a bewildered stare, 265
Four sturdy lictors put their necks beneath the curule chair;
And fourscore clients on the left, and fourscore on the right,
Arrayed themselves with swords and staves, and loins girt up for fight.
But, though without or staff or sword, so furious was the throng,
That scarce the train with might and main could bring their lord along. 270

They sent the haughtiest Claudius with shivered fasces home.
But what their care bequeathed us our madness flung away:
All the ripe fruit of threescore years was blighted in a day.
Exult, ye proud Patricians! The hard-fought fight is o'er.
We strove for honors — 'twas in vain; for freedom — 'tis no more.
No crier to the polling summons the eager throng;
No tribune breathes the word of might that guards the weak from wrong.
Our very hearts, that were so high, sink down beneath your will.
Riches, and lands, and power, and state — ye have them — keep them still.
Still keep the holy fillets; still keep the purple gown,
The axes, and the curule chair, the car, and laurel crown:
Still press us for your cohorts, and, when the fight is done,
Still fill your garners from the soil which our good swords have won.

Still, like a spreading ulcer, which leech-craft may not cure, 119
Let your foul usance eat away the substance of the poor.
Still let your haggard debtors bear all their fathers bore;
Still let your dens of torment be noisome as of yore;
No fire when Tiber freezes; no air in dog-star heat;
And store of rods for free-born backs, and holes for free-born feet.
Heap heavier still the fetters; bar closer still the grate;
Patient as sheep we yield us up unto your cruel hate. 126
But, by the Shades beneath us, and by the gods above,
Add not unto your cruel hate your yet more cruel love!
Have ye not graceful ladies, whose spotless lineage springs
From Consuls, and High Pontiffs, and ancient Alban kings? 130
Ladies, who deign not on our paths to set their tender feet,
Who from their cars look down with scorn upon the wondering street,
Who in Corinthian mirrors their own proud smiles behold,
And breathe of Capuan odors, and shine with Spanish gold?
Then leave the poor Plebeian his single tie to life — 135

The sweet, sweet love of daughter, of sister, and of wife,
The gentle speech, the balm for all that his vexed soul endures,
The kiss, in which he half forgets even such a yoke as yours.
Still let the maiden's beauty swell the father's breast with pride;
Still let the bridegroom's arms infold an unpolluted bride. 140
Spare us the inexpiable wrong, the unutterable shame,
That turns the coward's heart to steel, the sluggard's blood to flame,
Lest, when our latest hope is fled, ye taste of our despair,
And learn by proof, in some wild hour, how much the wretched dare."

Straightway Virginius led the maid a little space aside, 145
To where the reeking shambles stood, piled up with horn and hide,
Close to yon low dark archway, where, in a crimson flood,
Leaps down to the great sewer the gurgling stream of blood.

Hard by, a flesher on a block had laid his whittle down;
Virginius caught the whittle up, and hid it in his gown.
And then his eyes grew very dim, and his throat began to swell, 151
And in a hoarse, changed voice he spake, "Farewell, sweet child! Farewell!
Oh! how I loved my darling! Though stern I sometimes be,
To thee, thou know'st, I was not so. Who could be so to thee?
And how my darling loved me! How glad she was to hear 155
My footstep on the threshold when I came back last year!
And how she danced with pleasure to see my civic crown,
And took my sword, and hung it up, and brought me forth my gown!
Now, all those things are over — yes, all thy pretty ways,
Thy needlework, thy prattle, thy snatches of old lays; 160
And none will grieve when I go forth, or smile when I return,
Or watch beside the old man's bed, or weep upon his urn.
The house that was the happiest within the Roman walls,

The house that envied not the wealth of Capua's marble halls,
Now, for the brightness of thy smile, must have eternal gloom, 165
And for the music of thy voice, the silence of the tomb.
The time is come. See how he points his eager hand this way!
See how his eyes gloat on thy grief, like a kite's upon the prey!
With all his wit, he little deems, that, spurned, betrayed, bereft,
Thy father hath in his despair one fearful refuge left. 170
He little deems that in this hand I clutch what still can save
Thy gentle youth from taunts and blows, the portion of the slave;
Yea, and from nameless evil, that passeth taunt and blow —
Foul outrage which thou knowest not, which thou shalt never know.
Then clasp me round the neck once more, and give me one more kiss; 175
And now, mine own dear little girl, there is no way but this."

I

With that he lifted high the steel, and smote her in the side,
And in her blood she sank to earth, and with one sob she died.

Then, for a little moment, all people held their breath;
And through the crowded Forum was stillness as of death; 180
And in another moment brake forth from one and all
A cry as if the Volscians were coming o'er the wall.
Some with averted faces shrieking fled home amain;
Some ran to call a leech; and some ran to lift the slain;
Some felt her lips and little wrist, if life might there be found; 185
And some tore up their garments fast, and strove to stanch the wound.
In vain they ran, and felt, and stanched; for never truer blow
That good right arm had dealt in fight against a Volscian foe.

When Appius Claudius saw that deed, he shuddered and sank down,
And hid his face some little space with the corner of his gown, 190

Till, with white lips and bloodshot eyes, Virginius tottered nigh,
And stood before the judgment-seat, and held the knife on high.
"Oh! dwellers in the nether gloom, avengers of the slain,
By this dear blood I cry to you, do right between us twain;
And even as Appius Claudius hath dealt by me and mine,
Deal you by Appius Claudius and all the Claudian line!"
So spake the slayer of his child, and turned, and went his way;
But first he cast one haggard glance to where the body lay,
And writhed, and groaned a fearful groan, and then, with steadfast feet
Strode right across the market-place unto the Sacred Street.

Then up sprang Appius Claudius: "Stop him; alive or dead!
Ten thousand pounds of copper to the man who brings his head."

He looked upon his clients; but none would work his will.

He looked upon his lictors; but they trembled, and stood still.

And as Virginius through the press his way in silence cleft, 205

Ever the mighty multitude fell back to right and left.

And he hath passed in safety unto his woeful home,

And there ta'en horse to tell the camp what deeds are done in Rome.

By this the flood of people was swollen from every side,

And streets and porches round were filled with that o'erflowing tide; 210

And close around the body gathered a little train

Of them that were the nearest and dearest to the slain.

They brought a bier, and hung it with many a cypress crown,

And gently they uplifted her, and gently laid her down.

The face of Appius Claudius wore the Claudian scowl and sneer, 215

And in the Claudian note he cried, "What doth this rabble here?

Have they no crafts to mind at home, that hitherward they stray?
Ho! lictors, clear the market-place, and fetch the corpse away!"
The voice of grief and fury till then had not been loud;
But a deep, sullen murmur wandered among the crowd 220
Like the moaning noise that goes before the whirlwind on the deep,
Or the growl of a fierce watch-dog but half-aroused from sleep.
But when the lictors at that word, tall yeomen all and strong
Each with his axe and sheaf of twigs, went down into the throng,
Those old men say, who saw that day of sorrow and of sin, 225
That in the Roman Forum was never such a din.
The wailing, hooting, cursing, the howls of grief and hate,
Were heard beyond the Pincian Hill, beyond the Latin Gate.
But close around the body, where stood the little train
Of them that were the nearest and dearest to the slain,

No cries were there, but teeth set fast, low whispers and
    black frowns,   231
And breaking up of benches, and girding up of gowns.
'Twas well the lictors might not pierce to where the
    maiden lay,
Else surely had they been all twelve torn limb from limb
    that day.
Right glad they were to struggle back, blood streaming
    from their heads,   235
With axes all in splinters, and raiment all in shreds.
Then Appius Claudius gnawed his lip, and the blood left
    his cheek,
And thrice he beckoned with his hand, and thrice he
    strove to speak;
And thrice the tossing Forum set up a frightful yell:
"See, see, thou dog! what thou hast done; and hide thy
    shame in hell!   240
Thou that wouldst make our maidens slaves must first
    make slaves of men.
Tribunes! Hurrah for Tribunes! Down with the
    wicked Ten!"
And straightway, thick as hailstones, came whizzing
    through the air,
Pebbles, and bricks, and potsherds, all round the curule
    chair:

Twelve times the crowd made at him; five times they seized his gown;
Small chance was his to rise again, if once they got him down:
And sharper came the pelting; and evermore the yell—
"Tribunes! we will have Tribunes!"—rose with a louder swell:
And the chair tossed as tosses a bark with tattered sail 275
When raves the Adriatic beneath an eastern gale,
When the Calabrian sea-marks are lost in clouds of spume,
And the great Thunder-Cape has donned his veil of inky gloom.
One stone hit Appius in the mouth, and one beneath the ear;
And ere he reached Mount Palatine, he swooned with pain and fear. 280
His cursed head, that he was wont to hold so high with pride,
Now, like a drunken man's, hung down, and swayed from side to side;
And when his stout retainers had brought him to his door,

His face and neck were all one cake of filth and clotted
   gore.
As Appius Claudius was that day, so may his grandson
   be!   285
God send Rome one such other sight, and send me there
   to see!

THE PROPHECY OF CAPYS

A LAY SUNG AT THE BANQUET IN THE CAPITOL, ON THE DAY WHEREON MANIUS CURIUS DENTATUS, A SECOND TIME CONSUL, TRIUMPHED OVER KING PYRRHUS AND THE TARENTINES, IN THE YEAR OF THE CITY CCCLXXIX

I

Now slain is King Amulius,
    Of the great Sylvian line,
Who reigned in Alba Longa,
    On the throne of Aventine.
Slain is the Pontiff Camers,
    Who spake the words of doom:
"The children to the Tiber,
    The mother to the tomb."

II

In Alba's lake no fisher
    His net to-day is flinging:
On the dark rind of Alba's oaks
    To-day no axe is ringing;

> The yoke hangs o'er the manger,
> > The scythe lies in the hay:
> Through all the Alban villages
> > No work is done to-day.

III

> And every Alban burgher
> > Hath donned his whitest gown;
> And every head in Alba
> > Weareth a poplar crown;
> And every Alban door-post
> > With boughs and flowers is gay;
> For to-day the dead are living,
> > The lost are found to-day.

IV

> They were doomed by a bloody king,
> > They were doomed by a lying priest,
> They were cast on the raging flood,
> > They were tracked by the raging beast;
> Raging beast and raging flood,
> > Alike have spared the prey:
> And to-day the dead are living,
> > The lost are found to-day.

V

The troubled river knew them,
  And smoothed his yellow foam,
And gently rocked the cradle
  That bore the fate of Rome.
The ravening she-wolf knew them,
  And licked them o'er and o'er,
And gave them of her own fierce milk,
  Rich with raw flesh and gore.
Twenty winters, twenty springs,
  Since then have rolled away;
And to-day the dead are living:
  The lost are found to-day.

VI

Blithe it was to see the twins,
  Right goodly youths and tall,
Marching from Alba Longa
  To their old grandsire's hall.
Along their path fresh garlands
  Are hung from tree to tree:
Before them stride the pipers,
  Piping a note of glee.

VII

On the right goes Romulus
 With arms to the elbows red,
And in his hand a broadsword, 55
 And on the blade a head —
A head in an iron helmet,
 With horse-hair hanging down,
A shaggy head, a swarthy head,
 Fixed in a ghastly frown — 60
The head of King Amulius
 Of the great Sylvian line,
Who reigned in Alba Longa,
 On the throne of Aventine.

VIII

On the left side goes Remus, 65
 With wrists and fingers red,
And in his hand a boar-spear,
 And on the point a head —
A wrinkled head and aged,
 With silver beard and hair, 70
And holy fillets round it,
 Such as the pontiffs wear —

The head of ancient Camers,
  Who spake the words of doom:
"The children to the Tiber,
  The mother to the tomb."

IX

Two and two behind the twins
  Their trusty comrades go,
Four-and-forty valiant men,
  With club, and axe, and bow.
On each side every hamlet
  Pours forth its joyous crowd,
Shouting lads and baying dogs,
  And children laughing loud,
And old men weeping fondly
  As Rhea's boys go by,
And maids who shriek to see the heads,
  Yet, shrieking, press more nigh.

X

So they marched along the lake;
  They marched by fold and stall,
By corn-field and by vineyard,
  Unto the old man's hall.

XI

In the hall-gate sat Capys,°
    Capys, the sightless seer;
From head to foot he trembled   95
    As Romulus drew near.
And up stood stiff his thin white hair,
    And his blind eyes flashed fire:
"Hail! foster child of the wondrous nurse!
    Hail! son of the wondrous sire!   100

XII

"But thou — what dost thou here
    In the old man's peaceful hall?
What doth the eagle in the coop,
    The bison in the stall?
Our corn fills many a garner;   105
    Our vines clasp many a tree;
Our flocks are white on many a hill;
    But these are not for thee.

XIII

"For thee no treasure ripens
    In the Tartessian mine;   110
For thee no ship brings precious bales
    Across the Libyan brine;

Thou shalt not drink from amber;
  Thou shalt not rest on down;
Arabia shall not steep thy locks,   115
  Nor Sidon tinge thy gown.

XIV

" Leave gold and myrrh and jewels,
  Rich table and soft bed,
To them who of man's seed are born,
  Whom woman's milk has fed.   120
Thou wast not made for lucre,
  For pleasure nor for rest;
Thou that art sprung from the War-god's loins
  And hast tugged at the she-wolf's breast.

XV

" From sunrise unto sunset   125
  All earth shall hear thy fame:
A glorious city thou shalt build,
  And name it by thy name:
And there, unquenched through ages,
  Like Vesta's sacred fire,   130
Shall live the spirit of thy nurse,
  The spirit of thy sire.

XVI

"The ox toils through the furrow,
  Obedient to the goad;
The patient ass, up flinty paths,　　　　135
  Plods with his weary load;
With whine and bound the spaniel
  His master's whistle hears;
And the sheep yields her patiently
  To the loud clashing shears.　　　　140

XVII

"But thy nurse will hear no master;
  Thy nurse will bear no load;
And woe to them that shear her,
  And woe to them that goad!
When all the pack, loud baying,　　　　145
  Her bloody lair surrounds,
She dies in silence, biting hard,
  Amidst the dying hounds.

XVIII

"Pomona loves the orchard;
  And Liber° loves the vine;　　　　150
And Pales loves the straw-built shed
  Warm with the breath of kine;

And Venus loves the whispers
  Of plighted youth and maid,
In April's ivory moonlight
  Beneath the chestnut shade.

XIX

" But thy father loves the clashing
  Of broadsword and of shield:
He loves to drink the stream that reeks
  From the fresh battle-field:
He smiles a smile more dreadful
  Than his own dreadful frown,
When he sees the thick black cloud of smoke
  Go up from the conquered town.

XX

" And such as is the War-god,
  The author of thy line
And such as she who suckled thee,
  Even such be thou and thine.
Leave to the soft Campanian
  His baths and his perfumes;
Leave to the sordid race of Tyre
  Their dyeing-vats and looms;

Leave to the sons of Carthage
　　The rudder and the oar;
Leave to the Greek his marble Nymphs
　　And scrolls of wordy lore.

XXI

" Thine, Roman, is the pilum°:
　　Roman, the sword is thine,
The even trench, the bristling mound,
　　The legion's ordered line;
And thine the wheels of triumph,
　　Which, with their laurelled train,
Move slowly up the shouting streets
　　To Jove's eternal fane.

XXII

" Beneath thy yoke the Volscian
　　Shall vail his lofty brow:
Soft Capua's curled revellers
　　Before thy chairs shall bow:
The Lucumoes of Arnus
　　Shall quake thy rods to see;
And the proud Samnite's heart of steel
　　Shall yield to only thee

XXIII

"The Gaul shall come against thee
　From the land of snow and night:
Thou shalt give his fair-haired armies
　To the raven and the kite.

XXIV

"The Greek shall come against thee,
　The conqueror of the East.
Beside him stalks to battle
　The huge earth-shaking beast,
The beast on whom the castle
　With all its guards doth stand,
The beast who hath between his eyes
　The serpent for a hand.
First march the bold Epirotes,
　Wedged close with shield and spear;
And the ranks of false Tarentum
　Are glittering in the rear.

XXV

"The ranks of false Tarentum
　Like hunted sheep shall fly:
In vain the bold Epirotes°
　Shall round their standards die:

And Apennine's gray vultures
　　Shall have a noble feast
On the fat and the eyes　　　　　　　　　　215
　　Of the huge earth-shaking beast.

XXVI

" Hurrah ! for the good weapons
　　That keep the War-god's land.
Hurrah ! for Rome's stout pilum
　　In a stout Roman hand.　　　　　　　220
Hurrah ! for Rome's short broadsword,
　　That through the thick array
Of levelled spears and serried shields
　　Hews deep its gory way.

XXVII

" Hurrah ! for the great triumph　　　　225
　　That stretches many a mile.
Hurrah ! for the wan captives
　　That pass in endless file.
Ho ! bold Epirotes, whither
　　Hath the Red King° ta'en flight?　　230
Ho ! dogs of false Tarentum,
　　Is not the gown washed white?

XXVIII

"Hurrah! for the great triumph
  That stretches many a mile.
Hurrah! for the rich dye of Tyre,
  And the fine web of Nile,
The helmets gay with plumage
  Torn from the pheasant's wings,
The belts set thick with starry gems
  That shone on Indian kings,
The urns of massy silver,
  The goblets rough with gold,
The many-colored tablets bright
  With loves and wars of old,
The stone that breathes and struggles,
  The brass that seems to speak; —
Such cunning they who dwell on high
  Have given unto the Greek.

XXIX

"Hurrah! for Manius Curius,
  The bravest son of Rome,
Thrice in utmost need sent forth,
  Thrice drawn in triumph home.

Weave, weave, for Manius Curius
    The third embroidered gown:
Make ready the third lofty car,   255
    And twine the third green crown;
And yoke the steeds of Rosea
    With necks like a bended bow,
And deck the bull, Mevania's bull,
    The bull as white as snow.   260

XXX

"Blest and thrice blest the Roman
    Who sees Rome's brightest day,
Who sees that long victorious pomp
    Wind down the Sacred Way,
And through the bellowing Forum   265
    And round the Suppliant's Grove,°
Up to the everlasting gates
    Of Capitolian Jove.

XXXI

"Then where, o'er two bright havens,
    The towers of Corinth frown;   270
Where the gigantic King of Day
    On his own Rhodes looks down;

Where soft Orontes murmurs
   Beneath the laurel shades;
Where Nile reflects the endless length   275
   Of dark-red colonnades;
Where in the still deep water,
   Sheltered from waves and blasts,
Bristles the dusky forest
   Of Byrsa's thousand masts;   280
Where fur-clad hunters wander
   Amidst the northern ice;
Where through the sand of morning-land
   The camel bears the spice;
Where Atlas flings his shadow   285
   Far o'er the western foam,
Shall be great fear on all who hear
   The mighty name of Rome."

THE RAVEN

Once upon a midnight dreary, while I pondered, weak and weary,
Over many a quaint and curious volume of forgotten lore —
While I nodded, nearly napping, suddenly there came a tapping
As of some one gently rapping, rapping at my chamber door.
" 'Tis some visitor," I muttered, " tapping at my chamber door: 5
    Only this and nothing more."

Ah, distinctly I remember it was in the bleak December,
And each separate dying ember wrought its ghost upon the floor.
Eagerly I wished the morrow; — vainly I had sought to borrow
From my books surcease of sorrow — sorrow for the lost Lenore —   10

For the rare and radiant maiden whom the angels name
    Lenore :
        Nameless here for evermore.

And the silken sad uncertain rustling of each purple
    curtain
Thrilled me — filled me with fantastic terrors never
    felt before;
So that now, to still the beating of my heart, I stood
    repeating   15
" 'Tis some visitor entreating entrance at my chamber
    door,
Some late visitor entreating entrance at my chamber
    door :°
        This it is and nothing more."

Presently my soul grew stronger; hesitating then no
    longer,
" Sir," said I, " or Madam, truly your forgiveness I
    implore ;   20
But the fact is I was napping, and so gently you came
    rapping,
And so faintly you came tapping, tapping at my chamber door,

That I scarce was sure I heard you " — here I opened
  wide the door :
        Darkness there and nothing more.

Deep into that darkness peering, long I stood there
  wondering, fearing,   25
Doubting, dreaming dreams no mortals ever dared to
  dream before ;
But the silence was unbroken, and the stillness gave
  no token,
And the only word there spoken was the whispered
  word, " Lenore ! " —
This I whispered, and an echo murmured back the word,
  " Lenore ! "
        Merely this and nothing more.   30

Back into the chamber turning, all my soul within me
  burning,
Soon again I heard a tapping somewhat louder than
  before.
" Surely," said I, " surely that is something at my win-
  dow lattice ;
Let me see, then, what thereat is, and this mystery
  explore ;

Let my heart be still a moment and this mystery explore: 35
> 'Tis the wind and nothing more."

Open here I flung the shutter, when, with many a flirt and flutter
In there stepped a stately Raven° of the saintly days of yore.
Not the least obeisance made he; not a minute stopped or stayed he;
But, with mien of lord or lady, perched above my chamber door, 40
Perched upon a bust of Pallas° just above my chamber door:
> Perched, and sat, and nothing more.

Then this ebony bird beguiling my sad fancy into smiling,
By the grave and stern decorum of the countenance it wore, —
"Though thy crest be shorn and shaven, thou," I said, "art sure no craven, 45
Ghastly grim and ancient Raven wandering from the Nightly shore:

Tell me what thy lordly name is on the Night's Plutonian shore!"
> Quoth the Raven, "Nevermore."

Much I marvelled this ungainly fowl to hear discourse so plainly,
Though its answer little meaning — little relevancy bore;
For we cannot help agreeing that no living human being
Ever yet was blessed with seeing bird above his chamber door,
Bird or beast upon the sculptured bust above his chamber door,
> With such name as "Nevermore."

But the Raven, sitting lonely on that placid bust, spoke only
That one word, as if his soul in that one word he did outpour.
Nothing further then he uttered; not a feather then he fluttered,
Till I scarcely more than muttered, — "Other friends have flown before;
On the morrow *he* will leave me, as my Hopes have flown before."
> Then the bird said, "Nevermore."

Startled at the stillness broken by reply so aptly spoken,
"Doubtless," said I, "what it utters is its only stock and store,
Caught from some unhappy master whom unmerciful Disaster
Followed fast and followed faster till his songs one burden bore:
Till the dirges of his Hope that melancholy burden° bore
    Of 'Never — nevermore.'"

But the Raven still beguiling all my fancy into smiling,
Straight I wheeled a cushioned seat in front of bird and bust and door;
Then, upon the velvet sinking, I betook myself to linking
Fancy unto fancy, thinking what this ominous bird of yore,
What this grim, ungainly, ghastly, gaunt, and ominous bird of yore
    Meant in croaking, "Nevermore."

Thus I sat engaged in guessing, but no syllable expressing
To the fowl whose fiery eyes now burned into my bosom's core;

This and more I sat divining, with my head at ease reclining
On the cushion's velvet lining that the lamplight gloated o'er,
But whose velvet violet lining with the lamplight gloating o'er
    She shall press, ah, nevermore.

Then, methought, the air grew denser, perfumed from an unseen censer
Swung by Seraphim whose footfalls tinkled on the tufted floor.
"Wretch," I cried, "thy God hath lent thee — by these angels he hath sent thee
Respite — respite and nepenthe from thy memories of Lenore!
Quaff, oh, quaff this kind nepenthe and forget this lost Lenore!"
    Quoth the Raven, "Nevermore."

"Prophet!" said I, "thing of evil! — prophet still, if bird or devil! —
Whether Tempter sent, or whether tempest tossed thee here ashore,

Desolate yet all undaunted, on this desert land enchanted —
On this home by Horror haunted — tell me truly, I implore —
Is there — is there balm in Gilead°? — tell me — tell me, I implore!"
        Quoth the Raven, "Nevermore."   90

"Prophet!" said I, "thing of evil — prophet still, if bird or devil!
By that Heaven that bends above us — by that God we both adore,
Tell this soul with sorrow laden if, within the distant Aidenn,°
It shall clasp a sainted maiden whom the angels name Lenore —
Clasp a rare and radiant maiden whom the angels name Lenore."   95
        Quoth the Raven, "Nevermore."

"Be that word our sign of parting, bird or fiend!" I shrieked, upstarting:
"Get thee back into the tempest and the Night's Plutonian shore!

Leave no black plume as a token of that lie thy soul hath spoken!
Leave my loneliness unbroken! — quit the bust above my door! 100
Take thy beak from out my heart, and take thy form from off my door!"
        Quoth the Raven, "Nevermore."

And the Raven, never flitting, still is sitting, still is sitting
On the pallid bust of Pallas just above my chamber door;
And his eyes have all the seeming of a demon's that is dreaming, 105
And the lamplight o'er him streaming throws his shadow on the floor;
And my soul from out that shadow that lies floating on the floor
        Shall be lifted — Nevermore!

THE VISION OF SIR LAUNFAL

Prelude to Part First

Over his keys the musing organist,
  Beginning doubtfully and far away,
First lets his fingers wander as they list,
  And builds a bridge from Dreamland for his lay:
Then, as the touch of his loved instrument   5
  Gives hope and fervor, nearer draws his theme,
First guessed by faint auroral flushes sent
  Along the wavering vista of his dream.

Not only around our infancy°
Doth heaven with all its splendors lie;   10
Daily, with souls that cringe and plot,
We Sinais° climb and know it not.

Over our manhood bend the skies;
  Against our fallen and traitor lives
The great winds utter prophecies;   15
  With our faint hearts the mountain strives;

147

Its arms outstretched, the druid wood
    Waits with its benedicite;
And to our age's drowsy blood
    Still shouts the inspiring sea.

Earth gets its price for what Earth gives us;
    The beggar is taxed for a corner to die in,
The priest hath his fee who comes and shrives us,
    We bargain for the graves we lie in;
At the devil's booth are all things sold,
Each ounce of dross costs its ounce of gold;
    For a cap and bells our lives we pay,
Bubbles we buy with a whole soul's tasking:
    'Tis heaven alone that is given away,
'Tis only God may be had for the asking;
    No price is set on the lavish summer;
    June may be had by the poorest comer.

And what is so rare as a day in June?
    Then, if ever, come perfect days;
Then Heaven tries the earth if it be in tune,
    And over it softly her warm ear lays;
Whether we look, or whether we listen,
We hear life murmur, or see it glisten;

Every clod feels a stir of might,
  An instinct within it that reaches and towers,
And, groping blindly above it for light,
  Climbs to a soul in grass and flowers;
The flush of life may well be seen
  Thrilling back over hills and valleys;
The cowslip startles in meadows green,
  The buttercup catches the sun in its chalice,
And there's never a leaf nor a blade too mean
  To be some happy creature's palace;
The little bird sits at his door in the sun,
  Atilt like a blossom among the leaves,
And lets his illumined being o'errun
  With the deluge of summer it receives;
His mate feels the eggs beneath her wings,
And the heart in her dumb breast flutters and sings;
He sings to the wide world, and she to her nest, —
In the nice ear of Nature which song is the best?

Now is the high-tide of the year,
  And whatever of life hath ebbed away
Comes flooding back with a ripply cheer,
  Into every bare inlet and creek and bay;
Now the heart is so full that a drop overfills it,

We are happy now because God wills it;
No matter how barren the past may have been,
'Tis enough for us now that the leaves are green;
We sit in the warm shade and feel right well 65
How the sap creeps up and the blossoms swell;
We may shut our eyes, but we cannot help knowing
That skies are clear and grass is growing;
The breeze comes whispering in our ear,
That dandelions are blossoming near, 70
  That maize has sprouted, that streams are flowing,
That the river is bluer than the sky,
That the robin is plastering his house hard by;
And if the breeze kept the good news back,
For other couriers we should not lack; 75
  We could guess it all by yon heifer's lowing, —
And hark! how clear bold chanticleer,
Warmed with the new wine of the year,
  Tells all in his lusty crowing!

Joy comes, grief goes, we know not how; 80
Everything is happy now,
  Everything is upward striving;
'Tis as easy now for the heart to be true
As for grass to be green or skies to be blue, —
  'Tis the natural way of living: 85

Who knows whither the clouds have fled?
　In the unscarred heaven they leave no wake;
And the eyes forget the tears they have shed,
　The heart forgets its sorrow and ache;
The soul partakes of the season's youth,
　And the sulphurous rifts of passion and woe
Lie deep 'neath a silence pure and smooth,
Like burnt-out craters healed with snow.
What wonder if Sir Launfal now
Remembered the keeping of his vow?

Part First

I

" My golden spurs now bring to me,
　And bring to me my richest mail,
For to-morrow I go over land and sea
　In search of the Holy Grail;
Shall never a bed for me be spread,
Nor shall a pillow be under my head,
Till I begin my vow to keep;
Here on the rushes will I sleep,
And perchance there may come a vision true
Ere day create the world anew."

Slowly Sir Launfal's eyes grew dim,
Slumber fell like a cloud on him,
And into his soul the vision flew.

II

The crows flapped over by twos and threes,
In the pool drowsed the cattle up to their knees, 110
  The little birds sang as if it were
  The one day of summer in all the year,
And the very leaves seemed to sing on the trees:
The castle alone in the landscape lay
Like an outpost of winter, dull and gray; 115
'Twas the proudest hall in the North Countree,°
And never its gates might opened be,
Save to lord or lady of high degree;
Summer besieged it on every side,
But the churlish stone her assaults defied; 120
She could not scale the chilly wall,
Though round it for leagues her pavilions tall
Stretched left and right,
Over the hills and out of sight;
  Green and broad was every tent, 125
  And out of each a murmur went
Till the breeze fell off at night.

III

The drawbridge dropped with a surly clang,
And through the dark arch a charger sprang,
Bearing Sir Launfal, the maiden knight,
In his gilded mail, that flamed so bright
It seemed the dark castle had gathered all
Those shafts the fierce sun had shot over its wall
  In the siege of three hundred summers long,
And, binding them all in one blazing sheaf,
  Had cast them forth: so, young and strong,
And lightsome as a locust-leaf,
Sir Launfal flashed forth in his unscarred mail,
To seek in all climes for the Holy Grail.

IV

It was morning on hill and stream and tree,
  And morning in the young knight's heart;
Only the castle moodily
Rebuffed the gifts of the sunshine free,
  And gloomed by itself apart;
The season brimmed all other things up
Full as the rain fills the pitcher-plant's cup.

V

As Sir Launfal made morn through the darksome gate,
    He was 'ware of a leper, crouched by the same,
Who begged with his hand and moaned as he sate;
    And a loathing over Sir Launfal came; 150
The sunshine went out of his soul with a thrill,
    The flesh 'neath his armor 'gan shrink and crawl,
And midway its leap his heart stood still
    Like a frozen waterfall;
For this man, so foul and bent of stature, 155
Rasped harshly against his dainty nature,
And seemed the one blot on the summer morn, —
So he tossed him a piece of gold in scorn.

VI

The leper raised not the gold from the dust:
" Better to me the poor man's crust, 160
Better the blessing of the poor,
Though I turn me empty from his door;
That is no true alms which the hand can hold;
He gives nothing but worthless gold
    Who gives from a sense of duty; 165
But he who gives a slender mite,
And gives to that which is out of sight,

That thread of the all-sustaining Beauty
Which runs through all and doth all unite, —
The hand cannot clasp the whole of his alms,
The heart outstretches its eager palms,
For a god goes with it and makes it store
To the soul that was starving in darkness before.'

Prelude to Part Second°

Down swept the chill wind from the mountain peak,
   From the snow five thousand summers old;
On open wold and hill-top bleak
   It had gathered all the cold,
And whirled it like sleet on the wanderer's cheek;
It carried a shiver everywhere
From the unleafed boughs and pastures bare;
The little brook heard it and built a roof
'Neath which he could house him, winter-proof;
All night by the white stars' frosty gleams
He groined his arches and matched his beams;
Slender and clear were his crystal spars
As the lashes of light that trim the stars;
He sculptured every summer delight
In his halls and chambers out of sight;
Sometimes his tinkling waters slipt

Down through a frost-leaved forest-crypt, 190
Long, sparkling aisles of steel-stemmed trees
Bending to counterfeit a breeze;
Sometimes the roof no fretwork knew
But silvery mosses that downward grew;
Sometimes it was carved in sharp relief 195
With quaint arabesques of ice-fern leaf;
Sometimes it was simply smooth and clear
For the gladness of heaven to shine through, and here
He had caught the nodding bulrush-tops
And hung them thickly with diamond drops, 200
That crystalled the beams of moon and sun,
And made a star of every one:
No mortal builder's most rare device
Could match this winter-palace of ice;
'Twas as if every image that mirrored lay 205
In his depths serene through the summer day,
Each fleeting shadow of earth and sky,
   Lest the happy model should be lost,
Had been mimicked in fairy masonry
   By the elfin builders of the frost. 210

Within the hall are song and laughter,
   The cheeks of Christmas glow red and jolly,

And sprouting is every corbel and rafter
With lightsome green of ivy and holly;
Through the deep gulf of the chimney wide   215
Wallows the Yule-log's roaring tide;
The broad flame-pennons droop and flap
   And belly and tug as a flag in the wind;
Like a locust shrills the imprisoned sap,
   Hunted to death in its galleries blind;   220
And swift little troops of silent sparks,
   Now pausing, now scattering away as in fear,
Go threading the soot-forest's tangled darks,
   Like herds of startled deer.

But the wind without was eager and sharp,   225
Of Sir Launfal's gray hair it makes a harp,
    And rattles and wrings
    The icy strings,
  Singing, in dreary monotone,
  A Christmas carol of its own,   230
  Whose burden still, as he might guess,
  Was — "Shelterless, shelterless, shelterless!"
The voice of the seneschal flared like a torch
As he shouted the wanderer away from the porch,
And he sat in the gateway and saw all night   235

The great hall-fire, so cheery and bold,
Through the window-slits of the castle old,
Build out its piers of ruddy light
Against the drift of the cold.

PART SECOND

I

There was never a leaf on bush or tree, 240
The bare boughs rattled shudderingly;
The river was numb and could not speak,
For the weaver Winter° its shroud had spun;
A single crow on the tree-top bleak
From his shining feathers shed off the cold sun. 245
Again it was morning, but shrunk and cold,
As if her veins were sapless and old,
And she rose up decrepitly
For a last dim look at earth and sea.

II

Sir Launfal turned from his own hard gate, 250
For another heir in his earldom sate;
An old, bent man, worn out and frail,
He came back from seeking the Holy Grail;

Little he recked of his earldom's loss,
No more on his surcoat was blazoned the cross,   255
But deep in his soul the sign he wore,
The badge of the suffering and the poor.

III

Sir Launfal's raiment thin and spare
Was idle mail 'gainst the barbèd air,
For it was just at the Christmas time;   260
So he mused, as he sat, of a sunnier clime,
And sought for a shelter from cold and snow
In the light and warmth of long ago;
He sees the snake-like caravan crawl
O'er the edge of the desert, black and small,   265
Then nearer and nearer, till, one by one,
He can count the camels in the sun,
As over the red-hot sands they pass
To where, in its slender necklace of grass,
The little spring laughed and leapt in the shade,   270
And with its own self like an infant played,
And waved its signal of palms.

IV

"For Christ's sweet sake, I beg an alms;"
The happy camels may reach the spring,

But Sir Launfal sees only the gruesome thing, 275
The leper,° lank as the rain-blanched bone,
That cowers beside him, a thing as lone
And white as the ice-isles of Northern seas
In the desolate horror of his disease.

V

And Sir Launfal said, — " I behold in thee 280
An image of Him who died on the tree;
Thou also hast had thy crown of thorns, —
Thou also hast had the world's buffets and scorns, —
And to thy life were not denied
The wounds in the hands and feet and side; 285
Mild Mary's Son, acknowledge me;
Behold, through him, I give to Thee!"

VI

Then the soul of the leper stood up in his eyes
   And looked at Sir Launfal, and straightway he
Remembered in what a haughtier guise 290
   He had flung an alms to leprosie,°
When he girt his young life up in gilded mail
And set forth in search of the Holy Grail.
The heart within him was ashes and dust;
He parted in twain his single crust, 295

He broke the ice on the streamlet's brink,
And gave the leper to eat and drink;
'Twas a mouldy crust of coarse brown bread,
   'Twas water out of a wooden bowl, —
Yet with fine wheaten bread was the leper fed,   300
   And 'twas red wine he drank with his thirsty soul.

VII

As Sir Launfal mused with a downcast face,
A light shone round about the place;
The leper no longer crouched at his side,
But stood before him glorified,   305
Shining and tall and fair and straight
As the pillar that stood by the Beautiful Gate, —
Himself the Gate whereby men can
Enter the temple of God in Man.   309

VIII

His words were shed softer than leaves from the pine,
And they fell on Sir Launfal as snows on the brine,
Which mingle their softness and quiet in one
With the shaggy unrest they float down upon;
And the voice that was calmer than silence said,
" Lo, it is I, be not afraid !   315

In many climes, without avail,
Thou hast spent thy life for the Holy Grail;
Behold, it is here, — this cup which thou
Didst fill at the streamlet for me but now;
This crust is my body broken for thee,°   320
This water His blood that died on the tree;
The Holy Supper is kept, indeed,
In whatso we share with another's need, —
Not what we give, but what we share,
For the gift without the giver is bare;   325
Who gives himself with his alms feeds three, —
Himself, his hungering neighbor, and me."

IX

Sir Launfal awoke, as from a swound; —
"The Grail in my castle here is found!
Hang my idle armor up on the wall,   330
Let it be the spider's banquet-hall;
He must be fenced with stronger mail
Who would seek and find the Holy Grail."

X

The castle gate stands open now,
   And the wanderer is welcome to the hall   335
As the hangbird is to the elm tree bough;

THE VISION OF SIR LAUNFAL

No longer scowl the turrets tall,
The Summer's long siege at last is o'er;
When the first poor outcast went in at the door,
She entered with him in disguise,   340
And mastered the fortress by surprise;
There is no spot she loves so well on ground,
She lingers and smiles there the whole year round;
The meanest serf on Sir Launfal's land
Has hall and bower at his command;   345
And there's no poor man in the North Countree
But is lord of the earldom as much as he.

SOHRAB AND RUSTUM

AN EPISODE°

And the first grey of morning fill'd the east,
And the fog rose out of the Oxus° stream.
But all the Tartar camp along the stream
Was hush'd, and still the men were plunged in sleep;
Sohrab alone, he slept not; all night long 5
He had lain wakeful, tossing on his bed;
But when the grey dawn stole into his tent,
He rose, and clad himself, and girt his sword,
And took his horseman's cloak, and left his tent,
And went abroad into the cold wet fog, 10
Through the dim camp to Peran-Wisa's° tent.

Through the black Tartar tents he pass'd, which stood
Clustering like bee-hives on the low flat strand
Of Oxus, where the summer-floods o'erflow
When the sun melts the snows in high Pamere; 15
Through the black tents he pass'd, o'er that low strand,
And to a hillock came, a little back
From the stream's brink — the spot where first a boat,
Crossing the stream in summer, scrapes the land.

The men of former times had crown'd the top 20
With a clay fort; but that was fall'n, and now
The Tartars built there Peran-Wisa's tent,
A dome of laths, and o'er it felts were spread.
And Sohrab came there, and went in, and stood
Upon the thick piled carpets in the tent, 25
And found the old man sleeping on his bed
Of rugs and felts, and near him lay his arms.
And Peran-Wisa heard him, though the step
Was dull'd; for he slept light, an old man's sleep;
And he rose quickly on one arm, and said: — 30
 "Who art thou? for it is not yet clear dawn.
Speak! is there news, or any night alarm?"
 But Sohrab came to the bedside, and said: —
"Thou know'st me, Peran-Wisa! it is I.
The sun is not yet risen, and the foe 35
Sleep; but I sleep not; all night long I lie
Tossing and wakeful, and I come to thee.
For so did King Afrasiab bid me seek
Thy counsel, and to heed thee as thy son,
In Samarcand, before the army march'd; 40
And I will tell thee what my heart desires.
Thou know'st if, since from Ader-baijan first
I came among the Tartars and bore arms,

I have still served Afrasiab well, and shown,
At my boy's years, the courage of a man.   45
This too thou know'st, that while I still bear on
The conquering Tartar ensigns through the world,
And beat the Persians back on every field,
I seek one man, one man, and one alone —
Rustum, my father; who I hoped should greet,   50
Should one day greet, upon some well-fought field,
His not unworthy, not inglorious son.
So I long hoped, but him I never find.
Come then, hear now, and grant me what I ask.
Let the two armies rest to-day; but I   55
Will challenge forth the bravest Persian lords
To meet me, man to man; if I prevail,
Rustum will surely hear it; if I fall —
Old man, the dead need no one, claim no kin.
Dim is the rumor of a common fight,   60
Where host meets host, and many names are sunk;
But of a single combat fame speaks clear."°

   He spoke; and Peran-Wisa took the hand
Of the young man in his, and sigh'd, and said: —
   "O Sohrab, an unquiet heart is thine!   65
Canst thou not rest among the Tartar chiefs,
And share the battle's common chance with us

Who love thee, but must press for ever first,
In single fight incurring single risk,
To find a father thou hast never seen? 70
That were far best, my son, to stay with us
Unmurmuring; in our tents, while it is war,
And when 'tis truce, then in Afrasiab's towns.
But, if this one desire indeed rules all,
To seek out Rustum — seek him not through fight! 75
Seek him in peace, and carry to his arms,
O Sohrab, carry an unwounded son!
But far hence seek him, for he is not here.
For now it is not as when I was young,
When Rustum was in front of every fray; 80
But now he keeps apart, and sits at home,
In Seistan, with Zal, his father old.
Whether that his own mighty strength at last
Feels the abhorr'd approaches of old age,
Or in some quarrel with the Persian King. 85
There go! — Thou wilt not? Yet my heart forebodes
Danger or death awaits thee on this field.
Fain would I know thee safe and well, though lost
To us; fain therefore send thee hence, in peace
To seek thy father, not seek single fights 90
In vain; — but who can keep the lion's cub

From ravening, and who govern Rustum's son?
Go, I will grant thee what thy heart desires."

So said he, and dropp'd Sohrab's hand, and left
His bed, and the warm rugs whereon he lay; 95
And o'er his chilly limbs his woollen coat
He pass'd, and tied his sandals on his feet,
And threw a white cloak round him, and he took
In his right hand a ruler's staff, no sword;
And on his head he set his sheepskin cap, 100
Black, glossy, curl'd, the fleece of Kara-Kul;
And raised the curtain of his tent, and call'd
His herald to his side, and went abroad.

The sun by this had risen, and clear'd the fog
From the broad Oxus and the glittering sands. 105
And from their tents the Tartar horsemen filed
Into the open plain; so Haman bade —
Haman, who next to Peran-Wisa ruled
The host, and still was in his lusty prime.
From their black tents°, long files of horse they stream'd;
As when some grey November morn° the files, 111
In marching order spread, of long-neck'd cranes
Stream over Casbin and the southern slopes
Of Elburz, from the Aralian estuaries,
Or some frore Caspian reed-bed, southward bound 115

For the warm Persian sea-board — so they stream'd.
The Tartars of the Oxus, the King's guard,
First, with black sheepskin caps and with long spears;
Large men, large steeds; who from Bokhara come
And Khiva, and ferment the milk of mares. 120
Next, the more temperate Toorkmuns of the south,
The Tukas, and the lances of Salore,
And those from Attruck and the Caspian sands;
Light men and on light steeds, who only drink
The acrid milk of camels, and their wells. 125
And then a swarm of wandering horse, who came
From far, and a more doubtful service own'd;
The Tartars of Ferghana, from the banks
Of the Jaxartes, men with scanty beards
And close-set skull-caps; and those wilder hordes 130
Who roam o'er Kipchak and the northern waste,
Kalmucks and unkempt Kuzzaks, tribes who stray
Nearest the Pole, and wandering Kirghizzes,
Who come on shaggy ponies from Pamere;
These all filed out from camp into the plain. 135
And on the other side the Persians form'd; —
First a light cloud of horse, Tartars they seem'd,
The Ilyats of Khorassan; and behind,
The royal troops of Persia, horse and foot,

Marshall'd battalions bright in burnish'd steel. 140
But Peran-Wisa with his herald came,
Threading the Tartar squadrons to the front,
And with his staff kept back the foremost ranks.
And when Ferood, who led the Persians, saw
That Peran-Wisa kept the Tartars back, 145
He took his spear, and to the front he came,
And check'd his ranks, and fix'd them where they stood.
And the old Tartar came upon the sand
Betwixt the silent hosts, and spake, and said: —

"Ferood, and ye, Persians and Tartars, hear! 150
Let there be truce between the hosts to-day.
But choose a champion from the Persian lords
To fight our champion Sohrab, man to man."

As, in the country, on a morn in June,
When the dew glistens on the pearled ears, 155
A shiver runs through the deep corn for joy —
So, when they heard what Peran-Wisa said,
A thrill through all the Tartar squadrons ran
Of pride and hope for Sohrab, whom they loved.

But as a troop of pedlers, from Cabool, 160
Cross underneath the Indian Caucasus,
That vast sky-neighboring mountain of milk snow;
Crossing so high, that, as they mount, they pass

Long flocks of travelling birds dead on the snow,
Choked by the air, and scarce can they themselves
Slake their parch'd throats with sugar'd mulberries —
In single file they move, and stop their breath,
For fear they should dislodge the o'erhanging snows —
So the pale Persians held their breath with fear.

And to Ferood his brother chiefs came up
To counsel; Gudurz and Zoarrah came,
And Feraburz, who ruled the Persian host
Second, and was the uncle of the King;
These came and counsell'd, and then Gudurz said: —

"Ferood, shame bids us take their challenge up,
Yet champion have we none to match this youth.
He has the wild stag's foot, the lion's heart.
But Rustum came last night; aloof he sits
And sullen, and has pitch'd his tents apart.
Him will I seek, and carry to his ear
The Tartar challenge, and this young man's name.
Haply he will forget his wrath, and fight.
Stand forth the while, and take their challenge up."

So spake he; and Ferood stood forth and cried: —
"Old man, be it agreed as thou hast said!
Let Sohrab arm, and we will find a man."
He spake: and Peran-Wisa turn'd, and strode

Back through the opening squadrons to his tent.
But through the anxious Persians Gudurz ran, 189
And cross'd the camp which lay behind, and reach'd,
Out on the sands beyond it, Rustum's tents.
Of scarlet cloth they were, and glittering gay,
Just pitch'd; the high pavilion in the midst
Was Rustum's, and his men lay camp'd around.
And Gudurz enter'd Rustum's tent, and found 195
Rustum; his morning meal was done, but still
The table stood before him, charged with food —
A side of roasted sheep, and cakes of bread,
And dark green melons; and there Rustum sate
Listless, and held a falcon on his wrist, 200
And play'd with it; but Gudurz came and stood
Before him; and he look'd, and saw him stand,
And with a cry sprang up and dropp'd the bird,
And greeted Gudurz with both hands, and said: —

"Welcome! these eyes could see no better sight. 205
What news? but sit down first, and eat and drink."

But Gudurz stood in the tent-door, and said: —
"Not now! a time will come to eat and drink,
But not to-day; to-day has other needs.
The armies are drawn out, and stand at gaze; 210
For from the Tartars is a challenge brought

To pick a champion from the Persian lords
To fight their champion — and thou know'st his name —
Sohrab men call him, but his birth is hid.
O Rustum, like thy might is this young man's! 215
He has the wild stag's foot, the lion's heart;
And he is young, and Iran's chiefs are old,
Or else too weak; and all eyes turn to thee.
Come down and help us, Rustum, or we lose!"

    He spoke; but Rustum answer'd with a smile:— 220
" Go to! if Iran's chiefs are old, then I
Am older; if the young are weak, the King
Errs strangely; for the King, for Kai Khosroo,
Himself is young, and honors younger men,
And lets the aged moulder to their graves. 225
Rustum he loves no more, but loves the young —
The young may rise at Sohrab's vaunts, not I.
For what care I, though all speak Sohrab's fame?
For would that I myself had such a son,
And not that one slight helpless girl° I have — 230
A son so famed, so brave, to send to war,
And I to tarry with the snow-hair'd Zal,
My father, whom the robber Afghans vex,
And clip his borders short, and drive his herds,
And he has none to guard his weak old age. 235

There would I go, and hang my armor up,
And with my great name fence that weak old man,
And spend the goodly treasures I have got,
And rest my age, and hear of Sohrab's fame,
And leave to death the hosts of thankless kings,   240
And with these slaughterous hands draw sword no more."

  He spoke, and smiled; and Gudurz made reply: —
"What then, O Rustum, will men say to this,
When Sohrab dares our bravest forth, and seeks
Thee most of all, and thou, whom most he seeks,   245
Hidest thy face? Take heed lest men should say:
*Like some old miser, Rustum hoards his fame,
And shuns to peril it with younger men.*"

  And, greatly moved, then Rustum made reply: —
"O Gudurz, wherefore dost thou say such words?   250
Thou knowest better words than this to say.
What is one more, one less, obscure or famed,
Valiant or craven, young or old, to me?
Are not they mortal, am not I myself?
But who for men of nought would do great deeds?   255
Come, thou shalt see how Rustum hoards his fame!
But I will fight unknown, and in plain arms°;
Let not men say of Rustum, he was match'd
In single fight with any mortal man."

He spoke, and frown'd; and Gudurz turn'd, and ran
Back quickly through the camp in fear and joy — 261
Fear at his wrath, but joy that Rustum came.
But Rustum strode to his tent-door, and call'd
His followers in, and bade them bring his arms,
And clad himself in steel; the arms he chose 265
Were plain, and on his shield was no device,
Only his helm was rich, inlaid with gold,
And, from the fluted spine atop, a plume
Of horsehair waved, a scarlet horsehair plume.
So arm'd, he issued forth; and Ruksh, his horse, 270
Follow'd him like a faithful hound at heel —
Ruksh, whose renown was noised through all the earth,
The horse, whom Rustum on a foray once
Did in Bokhara by the river find
A colt beneath its dam, and drove him home, 275
And rear'd him; a bright bay, with lofty crest,
Dight with a saddle-cloth of broider'd green
Crusted with gold, and on the ground were work'd
All beasts of chase, all beasts which hunters know.
So follow'd, Rustum left his tents, and cross'd 280
The camp, and to the Persian host appear'd.
And all the Persians knew him, and with shouts
Hail'd; but the Tartars knew not who he was.

And dear as the wet diver to the eyes
Of his pale wife who waits and weeps on shore, 285
By sandy Bahrein, in the Persian Gulf,
Plunging all day in the blue waves, at night,
Having made up his tale of precious pearls,
Rejoins her in their hut upon the sands —
So dear to the pale Persians Rustum came. 290

And Rustum to the Persian front advanced,
And Sohrab arm'd in Haman's tent, and came.
And as afield the reapers cut a swath
Down through the middle of a rich man's corn,
And on each side are squares of standing corn, 295
And in the midst a stubble, short and bare —
So on each side were squares of men, with spears
Bristling, and in the midst, the open sand.
And Rustum came upon the sand, and cast
His eyes toward the Tartar tents, and saw 300
Sohrab come forth, and eyed him as he came.

As some rich woman, on a winter's morn,°
Eyes through her silken curtains the poor drudge
Who with numb blacken'd fingers makes her fire —
At cock-crow, on a starlit winter's morn, 305
When the frost flowers the whiten'd window-panes —
And wonders how she lives, and what the thoughts

Of that poor drudge may be; so Rustum eyed
The unknown adventurous youth, who from afar
Came seeking Rustum, and defying forth 310
All the most valiant chiefs; long he perused
His spirited air, and wonder'd who he was.
For very young he seem'd, tenderly rear'd;
Like some young cypress, tall, and dark, and straight,
Which in a queen's secluded garden throws 315
Its slight dark shadow on the moonlit turf,
By midnight, to a bubbling fountain's sound —
So slender Sohrab seem'd, so softly rear'd.
And a deep pity enter'd Rustum's soul
As he beheld him coming; and he stood, 320
And beckon'd to him with his hand, and said: —

"O thou young man,° the air of Heaven is soft,
And warm, and pleasant; but the grave is cold!
Heaven's air is better than the cold dead grave.
Behold me! I am vast, and clad in iron, 325
And tried; and I have stood on many a field
Of blood, and I have fought with many a foe —
Never was that field lost, or that foe saved.
O Sohrab, wherefore wilt thou rush on death?
Be govern'd! quit the Tartar host, and come 330
To Iran, and be as my son to me,

And fight beneath my banner till I die!
There are no youths in Iran brave as thou."

So he spake, mildly; Sohrab heard his voice,
The mighty voice of Rustum, and he saw
His giant figure planted on the sand,
Sole, like some single tower, which a chief
Hath builded on the waste in former years
Against the robbers; and he saw that head,
Streak'd with its first grey hairs; — hope filled his soul
And he ran forward and embraced his knees,
And clasp'd his hand within his own, and said: —

"O, by thy father's head! by thine own soul!
Art thou not Rustum? speak! art thou not he?"

But Rustum eyed askance the kneeling youth,
And turn'd away, and spake to his own soul: —

"Ah me, I muse what this young fox may mean!
False, wily, boastful, are these Tartar boys.
For if I now confess this thing he asks,
And hide it not, but say: Rustum is here!
He will not yield indeed, nor quit our foes,
But he will find some pretext not to fight,
And praise my fame, and proffer courteous gifts,
A belt or sword perhaps, and go his way.
And on a feast-tide, in Afrasiab's hall,

In Samarcand, he will arise and cry:
' I challenged once, when the two armies camp'd
Beside the Oxus, all the Persian lords
To cope with me in single fight; but they
Shrank, only Rustum dared; then he and I 360
Changed gifts, and went on equal terms away.'
So will he speak, perhaps, while men applaud;
Then were the chiefs of Iran shamed through me."

And then he turn'd, and sternly spake aloud: —
" Rise! wherefore dost thou vainly question thus 365
Of Rustum? I am here, whom thou hast call'd
By challenge forth; make good thy vaunt, or yield!
Is it with Rustum only thou wouldst fight?
Rash boy, men look on Rustum's face and flee!
For well I know, that did great Rustum stand 370
Before thy face this day, and were reveal'd,
There would be then no talk of fighting more.
But being what I am, I tell thee this —
Do thou record it in thine inmost soul:
Either thou shalt renounce thy vaunt and yield, 375
Or else thy bones shall strew this sand, till winds
Bleach them, or Oxus with his summer-floods,
Oxus in summer wash them all away."

He spoke; and Sohrab answer'd, on his feet: —

"Art thou so fierce? Thou wilt not fright me so! 380
I am no girl, to be made pale by words.
Yet this thou hast said well, did Rustum stand
Here on this field, there were no fighting then.
But Rustum is far hence, and we stand here.
Begin! thou art more vast, more dread than I, 385
And thou art proved, I know, and I am young —
But yet success sways with the breath of Heaven.
And though thou thinkest that thou knowest sure
Thy victory, yet thou canst not surely know.
For we are all, like swimmers in the sea, 390
Poised on the top of a huge wave of fate,
Which hangs uncertain to which side to fall.
And whether it will heave us up to land,
Or whether it will roll us out to sea,
Back out to sea, to the deep waves of death, 395
We know not, and no search will make us know;
Only the event will teach us in its hour."

He spoke, and Rustum answer'd not, but hurl'd
His spear; down from the shoulder, down it came,
As on some partridge in the corn a hawk, 400
That long has tower'd in the airy clouds,
Drops like a plummet; Sohrab saw it come,
And sprang aside, quick as a flash; the spear

Hiss'd, and went quivering down into the sand,
Which it sent flying wide; — then Sohrab threw   405
In turn, and full struck Rustum's shield; sharp rang,
The iron plates rang sharp, but turn'd the spear.
And Rustum seized his club, which none but he
Could wield; an unlopp'd trunk it was, and huge,
Still rough — like those which men in treeless plains
To build them boats fish from the flooded rivers,   411
Hyphasis or Hydaspes, when, high up
By their dark springs, the wind in winter-time
Hath made in Himalayan forests wrack,
And strewn the channels with torn boughs — so huge
The club which Rustum lifted now, and struck   416
One stroke; but again Sohrab sprang aside,
Lithe as the glancing snake, and the club came
Thundering to earth, and leapt from Rustum's hand.
And Rustum follow'd his own blow, and fell   420
To his knees, and with his fingers clutch'd the sand:
And now might Sohrab have unsheathed his sword,
And pierced the mighty Rustum while he lay
Dizzy, and on his knees, and choked with sand;
But he look'd on, and smiled, nor bared his sword,   425
But courteously drew back, and spoke, and said: —

"Thou strik'st too hard! that club of thine will float

Upon the summer-floods, and not my bones.
But rise, and be not wroth! not wroth am I;
No, when I see thee, wrath forsakes my soul. 430
Thou say'st, thou art not Rustum; be it so!
Who art thou then, that canst so touch my soul?
Boy as I am, I have seen battles too —
Have waded foremost in their bloody waves,
And heard their hollow roar of dying men; 435
But never was my heart thus touch'd before.
Are they from Heaven, these softenings of the heart?
O thou old warrior, let us yield to Heaven!
Come, plant we here in earth our angry spears,
And make a truce, and sit upon this sand, 440
And pledge each other in red wine, like friends,
And thou shalt talk to me of Rustum's deeds.
There are enough foes in the Persian host,
Whom I may meet, and strike, and feel no pang;
Champions enough Afrasiab has, whom thou 445
Mayst fight; fight them, when they confront thy spear!
But oh, let there be peace 'twixt thee and me!"

  He ceased, but while he spake, Rustum had risen,
And stood erect, trembling with rage; his club
He left to lie, but had regain'd his spear, 450
Whose fiery point now in his mail'd right-hand

Blazed bright and baleful, like that autumn-star,
The baleful sign of fevers; dust had soil'd
His stately crest, and dimm'd his glittering arms.   454
His breast heaved, his lips foam'd, and twice his voice
Was choked with rage; at last these words broke way:—
  "Girl! nimble with thy feet, not with thy hands!
Curl'd minion, dancer, coiner of sweet words!
Fight, let me hear thy hateful voice no more!
Thou art not in Afrasiab's gardens now   460
With Tartar girls, with whom thou art wont to dance;
But on the Oxus-sands, and in the dance
Of battle, and with me, who make no play
Of war; I fight it out, and hand to hand.
Speak not to me of truce, and pledge, and wine!   465
Remember all thy valor; try thy feints
And cunning! all the pity I had is gone;
Because thou hast shamed me before both the hosts
With thy light skipping tricks, and thy girl's wiles."
  He spoke, and Sohrab kindled at his taunts,   470
And he too drew his sword; at once they rush'd
Together, as two eagles on one prey
Come rushing down together from the clouds,
One from the east, one from the west; their shields
Dash'd with a clang together, and a din   475

Rose, such as that the sinewy woodcutters
Make often in the forest's heart at morn,
Of hewing axes, crashing trees — such blows
Rustum and Sohrab on each other hail'd,
And you would say that sun and stars took part   480
In that unnatural conflict; for a cloud
Grew suddenly in Heaven, and dark'd the sun
Over the fighters' heads; and a wind rose
Under their feet, and moaning swept the plain,
And in a sandy whirlwind wrapp'd the pair.   485
In gloom they twain were wrapp'd, and they alone;
For both the on-looking hosts on either hand
Stood in broad daylight, and the sky was pure,
And the sun sparkled on the Oxus stream.
But in the gloom they fought, with bloodshot eyes   490
And laboring breath; first Rustum struck the shield
Which Sohrab held stiff out; the steel-spiked spear
Rent the tough plates, but fail'd to reach the skin,
And Rustum pluck'd it back with angry groan.
Then Sohrab with his sword smote Rustum's helm,   495
Nor clove its steel quite through; but all the crest
He shore away, and that proud horsehair plume,
Never till now defiled, sank to the dust;
And Rustum bow'd his head; but then the gloom

Grew blacker, thunder rumbled in the air, 500
And lightnings rent the cloud; and Ruksh, the horse,
Who stood at hand, utter'd a dreadful cry; —
No horse's cry was that, most like the roar
Of some pain'd desert-lion, who all day
Hath trail'd the hunter's javelin in his side, 505
And comes at night to die upon the sand.
The two hosts heard that cry, and quaked for fear,
And Oxus curdled as it cross'd his stream.
But Sohrab heard, and quail'd not, but rush'd on,
And struck again; and again Rustum bow'd 510
His head; but this time all the blade, like glass,
Sprang in a thousand shivers on the helm,
And in the hand the hilt remain'd alone.
Then Rustum raised his head; his dreadful eyes
Glared, and he shook on high his menacing spear, 515
And shouted: *Rustum!* — Sohrab heard that shout,
And shrank amazed; back he recoil'd one step,
And scann'd with blinking eyes the advancing form;
And then he stood bewilder'd; and he dropp'd
His covering shield, and the spear pierced his side. 520
He reel'd, and staggering back, sank to the ground;
And then the gloom dispersed, and the wind fell,
And the bright sun broke forth, and melted all

The cloud; and the two armies saw the pair —
Saw Rustum standing, safe upon his feet, 525
And Sohrab, wounded, on the bloody sand.

    Then, with a bitter smile, Rustum began: —
"Sohrab, thou thoughtest in thy mind to kill
A Persian lord this day, and strip his corpse,
And bear thy trophies to Afrasiab's tent. 530
Or else that the great Rustum would come down
Himself to fight, and that thy wiles would move
His heart to take a gift, and let thee go.
And then that all the Tartar host would praise
Thy courage or thy craft, and spread thy fame, 535
To glad thy father in his weak old age.
Fool, thou art slain, and by an unknown man!
Dearer to the red jackals shalt thou be
Than to thy friends, and to thy father old."

    And, with a fearless mien, Sohrab replied: — 540
"Unknown thou art; yet thy fierce vaunt is vain.
Thou dost not slay me, proud and boastful man!
No! Rustum slays me, and this filial heart.
For were I match'd with ten such men as thee,
And I were that which till to-day I was, 545
They should be lying here, I standing there.
But that belovéd name unnerved my arm —

That name, and something, I confess, in thee,
Which troubles all my heart, and made my shield
Fall; and thy spear transfix'd an unarm'd foe. 550
And now thou boastest, and insult'st my fate.
But hear thou this, fierce man, tremble to hear:
The mighty Rustum shall avenge my death!
My father, whom I seek through all the world,
He shall avenge my death, and punish thee!" 555

    As when some hunter in the spring hath found
A breeding eagle sitting on her nest,
Upon the craggy isle of a hill-lake,
And pierced her with an arrow as she rose,
And follow'd her to find her where she fell 560
Far off;—anon her mate comes winging back
From hunting, and a great way off descries
His huddling young left sole; at that, he checks
His pinion, and with short uneasy sweeps
Circles above his eyry, with loud screams 565
Chiding his mate back to her nest; but she
Lies dying, with the arrow in her side,
In some far stony gorge out of his ken,
A heap of fluttering feathers—never more
Shall the lake glass her, flying over it; 570
Never the black and dripping precipices

Echo her stormy scream as she sails by —
As that poor bird flies home, nor knows his loss,
So Rustum knew not his own loss, but stood
Over his dying son, and knew him not. 575
  But, with a cold incredulous voice, he said: —
"What prate is this of fathers and revenge?
The mighty Rustum never had a son."
  And, with a failing voice, Sohrab replied: —
"Ah yes, he had! and that lost son am I. 580
Surely the news will one day reach his ear,
Reach Rustum, where he sits, and tarries long,
Somewhere, I know not where, but far from here;
And pierce him like a stab, and make him leap
To arms, and cry for vengeance upon thee. 585
Fierce man, bethink thee, for an only son!
What will that grief, what will that vengeance be?
Oh, could I live, till I that grief had seen!
Yet him I pity not so much, but her,
My mother, who in Ader-baijan dwells 590
With that old king, her father, who grows grey
With age, and rules over the valiant Koords.
Her most I pity, who no more will see
Sohrab returning from the Tartar camp,
With spoils and honor, when the war is done. 595

But a dark rumor will be bruited up,
From tribe to tribe, until it reach her ear;
And then will that defenceless woman learn
That Sohrab will rejoice her sight no more,
But that in battle with a nameless foe, 600
By the far-distant Oxus, he is slain."

He spoke; and as he ceased, he wept aloud,
Thinking of her he left, and his own death.
He spoke; but Rustum listen'd, plunged in thought.
Nor did he yet believe it was his son 605
Who spoke, although he call'd back names he knew;
For he had had sure tidings that the babe,
Which was in Ader-baijan born to him,
Had been a puny girl, no boy at all —
So that sad mother sent him word, for fear 610
Rustum should seek the boy, to train in arms —
And so he deem'd that either Sohrab took,
By a false boast, the style of Rustum's son;
Or that men gave it him, to swell his fame.
So deem'd he; yet he listen'd, plunged in thought 615
And his soul set to grief, as the vast tide
Of the bright rocking Ocean sets to shore
At the full moon; tears gather'd in his eyes;
For he remember'd his own early youth,

And all its bounding rapture; as, at dawn, 620
The shepherd from his mountain-lodge descries
A far, bright city, smitten by the sun,
Through many rolling clouds — so Rustum saw
His youth; saw Sohrab's mother, in her bloom;
And that old king, her father, who loved well 625
His wandering guest, and gave him his fair child
With joy; and all the pleasant life they led,
They three, in that long-distant summer-time —
The castle, and the dewy woods, and hunt
And hound, and morn on those delightful hills 630
In Ader-baijan. And he saw that Youth,
Of age and looks to be his own dear son,
Piteous and lovely, lying on the sand,
Like some rich hyacinth which by the scythe
Of an unskilful gardener has been cut, 635
Mowing the garden grass-plots near its bed,
And lies, a fragrant tower of purple bloom,
On the mown, dying grass — So Sohrab lay,
Lovely in death, upon the common sand.
And Rustum gazed on him with grief, and said: — 640
 "O Sohrab, thou indeed art such a son
Whom Rustum, wert thou his, might well have loved!
Yet here thou errest, Sohrab, or else men

SOHRAB AND RUSTUM

Have told thee false — thou art not Rustum's son.
For Rustum had no son; one child he had — 645
But one — a girl; who with her mother now
Plies some light female task, nor dreams of us —
Of us she dreams not, nor of wounds, nor war."

But Sohrab answer'd him in wrath; for now
The anguish of the deep-fix'd spear grew fierce, 650
And he desired to draw forth the steel,
And let the blood flow free, and so to die —
But first he would convince his stubborn foe;
And, rising sternly on one arm, he said: —

"Man, who art thou who dost deny my words? 655
Truth sits upon the lips of dying men,
And falsehood, while I lived, was far from mine.
I tell thee, prick'd upon this arm I bear
That seal which Rustum to my mother gave,
That she might prick it on the babe she bore." 660

He spoke; and all the blood left Rustum's cheeks,
And his knees totter'd, and he smote his hand
Against his breast, his heavy mailed hand,
That the hard iron corslet clank'd aloud;
And to his heart he press'd the other hand, 665
And in a hollow voice he spake, and said: —

"Sohrab, that were a proof which could not lie!

If thou show this, then art thou Rustum's son."

Then, with weak hasty fingers, Sohrab loosed
His belt, and near the shoulder bared his arm,
And show'd a sign in faint vermilion points
Prick'd; as a cunning workman, in Pekin,
Pricks with vermilion some clear porcelain vase,
An emperor's gift — at early morn he paints,
And all day long, and, when night comes, the lamp
Lights up his studious forehead and thin hands —
So delicately prick'd the sign appear'd
On Sohrab's arm, the sign of Rustum's seal.
It was that griffin, which of old rear'd Zal,
Rustum's great father, whom they left to die,
A helpless babe, among the mountain-rocks;
Him that kind creature found, and rear'd, and loved —
Then Rustum took it for his glorious sign.
And Sohrab bared that image on his arm,
And himself scann'd it long with mournful eyes,
And then he touch'd it with his hand and said: —

"How say'st thou? Is that sign the proper sign
Of Rustum's son, or of some other man's?"

He spoke; but Rustum gazed, and gazed, and stood
Speechless; and then he utter'd one sharp cry:
O boy — thy father! and his voice choked there.

And then a dark cloud pass'd before his eyes,
And his head swam, and he sank down to earth.
But Sohrab crawl'd to where he lay, and cast
His arms about his neck, and kiss'd his lips, 695
And with fond faltering fingers stroked his cheeks,
Trying to call him back to life; and life
Came back to Rustum, and he oped his eyes,
And they stood wide with horror; and he seized
In both his hands the dust which lay around, 700
And threw it on his head, and smirch'd his hair,
His hair, and face, and beard, and glittering arms;
And strong convulsive groanings shook his breast,
And his sobs choked him; and he clutch'd his sword,
To draw it, and for ever let life out. 705
But Sohrab saw his thought, and held his hands,
And with a soothing voice he spake, and said: —

"Father, forbear! for I but meet to-day
The doom which at my birth was written down 709
In Heaven, and thou art Heaven's unconscious hand.
Surely my heart cried out that it was thou,
When first I saw thee; and thy heart spoke too,
I know it! but fate trod those promptings down
Under its iron heel; fate, fate engaged
The strife, and hurl'd me on my father's spear. 715

But let us speak no more of this! I find
My father; let me feel that I have found!
Come, sit beside me on this sand, and take
My head betwixt thy hands, and kiss my cheeks,
And wash them with thy tears, and say: *My son!* 720
Quick! quick! for number'd are my sands of life,
And swift; for like the lightning to this field
I came, and like the wind I go away —
Sudden, and swift, and like a passing wind.
But it was writ in Heaven that this should be." 725

So said he, and his voice released the heart
Of Rustum, and his tears brake forth; he cast
His arms round his son's neck, and wept aloud,
And kiss'd him.   And awe fell on both the hosts,
When they saw Rustum's grief; and Ruksh, the horse,
With his head bowing to the ground and mane 731
Sweeping the dust, came near, and in mute woe
First to the one then to the other moved
His head, as if enquiring what their grief
Might mean; and from his dark, compassionate eyes,
The big warm tears roll'd down, and caked the sand. 736
But Rustum chid him with stern voice, and said: —

"Ruksh, now thou grievest; but, O Ruksh, thy feet
Should first have rotted on their nimble joints,

SOHRAB AND RUSTUM

Or ere they brought thy master to this field!" 740
   But Sohrab look'd upon the horse and said: —
"Is this, then, Ruksh? How often, in past days,
My mother told me of thee, thou brave steed,
My terrible father's terrible horse! and said,
That I should one day find thy lord and thee. 745
Come, let me lay my hand upon thy mane!
O Ruksh, thou art more fortunate than I;
For thou hast gone where I shall never go,
And snuff'd the breezes of my father's home.
And thou hast trod the sands of Seistan, 750
And seen the River of Helmund, and the Lake
Of Zirrah; and the aged Zal himself
Has often stroked thy neck, and given thee food,
Corn in a golden platter soak'd with wine,
And said: *O Ruksh! bear Rustum well!* — but I 755
Have never known my grandsire's furrow'd face,
Nor seen his lofty house in Seistan,
Nor slaked my thirst at the clear Helmund stream;
But lodged among my father's foes, and seen
Afrasiab's cities only, Samarcand, 760
Bokhara, and lone Khiva in the waste,
And the black Toorkmun tents; and only drunk
The desert rivers, Moorghab and Tejend,

Kohik, and where the Kalmuks feed their sheep,
The northern Sir; and this great Oxus stream,   765
The yellow Oxus, by whose brink I die."

    Then, with a heavy groan, Rustum bewailed: —
"Oh, that its waves were flowing over me!
Oh, that I saw its grains of yellow silt
Roll tumbling in the current o'er my head!"   770

    But, with a grave mild voice, Sohrab replied: —
"Desire not that, my father! thou must live.
For some are born to do great deeds, and live,
As some are born to be obscured, and die.
Do thou the deeds I die too young to do,   775
And reap a second glory in thine age;
Thou art my father, and thy gain is mine.
But come! thou seest this great host of men
Which follow me; I pray thee, slay not these!
Let me entreat for them; what have they done?   780
They follow'd me, my hope, my fame, my star.
Let them all cross the Oxus back in peace.
But me thou must bear hence, not send with them,
But carry me with thee to Seistan,
And place me on a bed, and mourn for me,   785
Thou, and the snow-hair'd Zal, and all thy friends.
And thou must lay me in that lovely earth,

And heap a stately mound above my bones,
And plant a far-seen pillar over all.
That so the passing horseman on the waste   790
May see my tomb a great way off, and cry:
Sohrab, the mighty Rustum's son, lies there,
Whom his great father did in ignorance kill!
And I be not forgotten in my grave."

   And, with a mournful voice, Rustum replied: —   795
" Fear not! as thou hast said, Sohrab, my son,
So shall it be; for I will burn my tents,
And quit the host, and bear thee hence with me,
And carry thee away to Seistan,
And place thee on a bed, and mourn for thee,   800
With the snow-headed Zal, and all my friends.
And I will lay thee in that lovely earth,
And heap a stately mound above thy bones,
And plant a far-seen pillar over all,
And men shall not forget thee in thy grave.   805
And I will spare thy host; yea, let them go!
Let them all cross the Oxus back in peace!
What should I do with slaying any more?
For would that all that I have ever slain
Might be once more alive; my bitterest foes,   810
And they who were call'd champions in their time,

And through whose death I won that fame I have —
And I were nothing but a common man,
A poor, mean soldier, and without renown,
So thou mightest live too, my son, my son! 815
Or rather would that I, even I myself,
Might now be lying on this bloody sand,
Near death, and by an ignorant stroke of thine,
Not thou of mine! and I might die, not thou;
And I, not thou, be borne to Seistan; 820
And Zal might weep above my grave, not thine;
And say: *O son, I weep thee not too sore,
For willingly, I know, thou met'st thine end!*
But now in blood and battles was my youth,
And full of blood and battles is my age, 825
And I shall never end this life of blood."

   Then, at the point of death, Sohrab replied: —
" A life of blood indeed, thou dreadful man°!
But thou shalt yet have peace; only not now,
Not yet! but thou shalt have it on that day, 830
When thou shalt sail in a high-masted ship,
Thou and the other peers of Kai Khosroo,
Returning home over the salt blue sea,
From laying thy dear master in his grave."

   And Rustum gazed in Sohrab's face, and said: — 835

"Soon be that day, my son, and deep that sea!
Till then, if fate so wills, let me endure."
  He spoke; and Sohrab smiled on him, and took
The spear, and drew it from his side, and eased
His wound's imperious anguish; but the blood   840
Came welling from the open gash, and life
Flow'd with the stream; — all down his cold white side
The crimson torrent ran, dim now and soil'd,
Like the soil'd tissue of white violets
Left, freshly gather'd, on their native bank,   845
By children whom their nurses call with haste
Indoors from the sun's eye; his head droop'd low,
His limbs grew slack; motionless, white, he lay —
White, with eyes closed; only when heavy gasps,
Deep heavy gasps quivering through all his frame, 850
Convulsed him back to life, he open'd them,
And fix'd them feebly on his father's face;
Till now all strength was ebb'd, and from his limbs
Unwillingly the spirit fled away,
Regretting the warm mansion which it left,   855
And youth, and bloom, and this delightful world.
  So, on the bloody sand, Sohrab lay dead;
And the great Rustum drew his horseman's cloak
Down o'er his face, and sate by his dead son.

As those black granite pillars, once high-rear'd   860
By Jemshid in Persepolis, to bear
His house, now 'mid their broken flights of steps
Lie prone, enormous, down the mountain side —
So in the sand lay Rustum by his son.

    And night came down over the solemn waste,   865
And the two gazing hosts, and that sole pair,
And darken'd all; and a cold fog, with night,
Crept from the Oxus. Soon a hum arose,
As of a great assembly loosed, and fires
Began to twinkle through the fog; for now   870
Both armies moved to camp, and took their meal;
The Persians took it on the open sands
Southward, the Tartars by the river marge;
And Rustum and his son were left alone.

    But the majestic river floated on,°   875
Out of the mist and hum of that low land,
Into the frosty starlight, and there moved,
Rejoicing, through the hush'd Chorasmian waste,
Under the solitary moon; — he flow'd
Right for the polar star, past Orgunjè,   880
Brimming, and bright, and large; then sands begin
To hem his watery march, and dam his streams,
And split his currents; that for many a league

The shorn and parcell'd Oxus strains along
Through beds of sand and matted rushy isles —   885
Oxus, forgetting the bright speed he had
In his high mountain-cradle in Pamere,
A foil'd circuitous wanderer — till at last
The long'd-for dash of waves is heard, and wide
His luminous home of waters opens, bright   890
And tranquil, from whose floor the new-bathed stars
Emerge, and shine upon the Aral Sea.

THE COURTSHIP OF MILES STANDISH

I

MILES STANDISH°

In the Old Colony days, in Plymouth the land of the Pilgrims,
To and fro in a room of his simple and primitive dwelling,
Clad in doublet and hose, and boots of Cordovan leather,
Strode, with a martial air, Miles Standish the Puritan Captain.
Buried in thought he seemed, with his hands behind him, and pausing 5
Ever and anon to behold his glittering weapons of warfare,
Hanging in shining array along the walls of the chamber, —
Cutlass and corselet of steel, and his trusty sword of Damascus,
Curved at the point and inscribed with its mystical Arabic sentence,

While underneath, in a corner, were fowling-piece, musket, and matchlock.
Short of stature he was, but strongly built and athletic,
Broad in the shoulders, deep-chested, with muscles and sinews of iron;
Brown as a nut was his face, but his russet beard was already
Flaked with patches of snow, as hedges sometimes in November.
Near him was seated John Alden,° his friend and household companion,
Writing with diligent speed at a table of pine by the window;
Fair-haired, azure-eyed, with delicate Saxon complexion,
Having the dew of his youth, and the beauty thereof, as the captives
Whom Saint Gregory saw, and exclaimed, "Not Angles but Angels."
Youngest of all was he of the men who came in the Mayflower.

Suddenly breaking the silence, the diligent scribe interrupting,

Spake, in the pride of his heart, Miles Standish the Captain of Plymouth.
"Look at these arms," he said, "the warlike weapons that hang here
Burnished and bright and clean, as if for parade or inspection!
This is the sword of Damascus I fought with in Flanders; this breastplate,   25
Well I remember the day! once saved my life in a skirmish;
Here in front you can see the very dint of the bullet
Fired point-blank at my heart by a Spanish arcabucero.°
Had it not been of sheer steel, the forgotten bones of Miles Standish
Would at this moment be mould, in their grave in the Flemish morasses."   30
Thereupon answered John Alden, but looked not up from his writing:
"Truly the breath of the Lord hath slackened the speed of the bullet;
He in his mercy preserved you, to be our shield and our weapon!"
Still the Captain continued, unheeding the words of the stripling:

"See, how bright they are burnished, as if in an arsenal hanging; 35
That is because I have done it myself, and not left it to others.
Serve yourself, would you be well served, is an excellent adage;
So I take care of my arms, as you of your pens and your inkhorn.
Then, too, there are my soldiers, my great, invincible army,
Twelve men, all equipped, having each his rest and his matchlock, 40
Eighteen shillings a month, together with diet and pillage,
And, like Cæsar, I know the name of each of my soldiers!"
This he said with a smile, that danced in his eyes, as the sunbeams
Dance on the waves of the sea, and vanish again in a moment.
Alden laughed as he wrote, and still the Captain continued: 45
"Look! you can see from this window my brazen howitzer planted

High on the roof of the church, a preacher who speaks to the purpose,
Steady, straightforward, and strong, with irresistible logic,
Orthodox, flashing conviction right into the hearts of the heathen.
Now we are ready, I think, for any assault of the Indians:
Let them come, if they like, and the sooner they try it the better, —
Let them come if they like, be it sagamore, sachem, or pow-wow,
Aspinet, Samoset, Corbitant, Squanto, or Tokamahamon!"

Long at the window he stood, and wistfully gazed on the landscape,
Washed with a cold grey mist, the vapory breath of the east-wind,
Forest and meadow and hill, and the steel-blue rim of the ocean,
Lying silent and sad, in the afternoon shadows and sunshine.
Over his countenance flitted a shadow like those on the landscape,

Gloom intermingled with light; and his voice was subdued with emotion,
Tenderness, pity, regret, as after a pause he proceeded: 60
"Yonder there, on the hill by the sea, lies buried Rose Standish;
Beautiful rose of love, that bloomed for me by the wayside!
She was the first to die of all who came in the Mayflower!
Green above her is growing the field of wheat we have sown there,
Better to hide from the Indian scouts the graves of our people, 65
Lest they should count them and see how many already have perished!"
Sadly his face he averted, and strode up and down, and was thoughtful.

Fixed to the opposite wall was a shelf of books, and among them
Prominent three, distinguished alike for bulk and for binding;
Barriffe's Artillery Guide, and the Commentaries of Cæsar, 70

Out of the Latin translated by Arthur Goldinge of London,
And, as if guarded by these, between them was standing the Bible,
Musing a moment before them, Miles Standish paused, as if doubtful
Which of the three he should choose for his consolation and comfort,
Whether the wars of the Hebrews, the famous campaigns of the Romans, 75
Or the Artillery practice, designed for belligerent Christians.
Finally down from its shelf he dragged the ponderous Roman,
Seated himself at the window, and opened the book, and in silence
Turned o'er the well-worn leaves, where thumb-marks thick on the margin,
Like the trample of feet, proclaimed the battle was hottest. 80
Nothing was heard in the room but the hurrying pen of the stripling,
Busily writing epistles important, to go by the Mayflower,

Ready to sail on the morrow, or next day at latest,
    God willing!
Homeward bound with the tidings of all that terrible
    winter,
Letters written by Alden, and full of the name of Pris-
    cilla,°   85
Full of the name and the fame of the Puritan maiden
    Priscilla!

II

LOVE AND FRIENDSHIP

Nothing was heard in the room but the hurrying pen
    of the stripling,
Or an occasional sigh from the laboring heart of the
    Captain,
Reading the marvellous words and achievements of
    Julius Cæsar.
After a while he exclaimed, as he smote with his hand
    palm downwards,   90
Heavily on the page: "A wonderful man was this
    Cæsar!
You are a writer, and I am a fighter, but here is a
    fellow

Who could both write and fight, and in both was equally
    skilful ! "
Straightway answered and spake John Alden, the
    comely, the youthful :
" Yes, he was equally skilled, as you say, with his pen
    and his weapons.   95
Somewhere have I read, but where I forget, he could
    dictate
Seven letters at once, at the same time writing his
    memoirs."
" Truly," continued the Captain, not heeding or hear-
    ing the other,
" Truly a wonderful man was Caius Julius Cæsar !
Better be first, he said, in a little Iberian village,   100
Than be second in Rome, and I think he was right when
    he said it.
Twice was he married before he was twenty, and many
    times after ;
Battles five hundred he fought, and a thousand cities
    he conquered ;
He, too, fought in Flanders, as he himself has re-
    corded ;
Finally he was stabbed by his friend, the orator Bru-
    tus !   105

Now, do you know what he did on a certain occasion in Flanders,
When the rear-guard of his army retreated, the front giving way too,
And the immortal Twelfth Legion was crowded so closely together
There was no room for their swords? Why, he seized a shield from a soldier,
Put himself straight at the head of his troops, and commanded the captains, 110
Calling on each by his name, to order forward the ensigns;
Then to widen the ranks, and give more room for their weapons;
So he won the day, the battle of something-or-other.
That's what I always say; if you wish a thing to be well done,
You must do it yourself, you must not leave it to others!" 115

All was silent again; the Captain continued his reading.
Nothing was heard in the room but the hurrying pen of the stripling

Writing epistles important to go next day by the Mayflower,
Filled with the name and the fame of the Puritan maiden Priscilla;
Every sentence began or closed with the name of Priscilla   120
Till the treacherous pen, to which he confided the secret,
Strove to betray it by singing and shouting the name of Priscilla!
Finally closing his book, with a bang of the ponderous cover,
Sudden and loud as the sound of a soldier grounding his musket,
Thus to the young man spake Miles Standish the Captain of Plymouth: 125
"When you have finished your work, I have something important to tell you.
Be not however in haste; I can wait; I shall not be impatient!"
Straightway Alden replied, as he folded the last of his letters,
Pushing his papers aside, and giving respectful attention:

" Speak; for whenever you speak, I am always ready
    to listen,   130
Always ready to hear whatever pertains to Miles Standish."
Thereupon answered the Captain, embarrassed, and culling his phrases:
" 'Tis not good for a man to be alone, say the Scriptures.
This I have said before, and again and again I repeat
    it;
Every hour in the day, I think it, and feel it, and say it.
Since Rose Standish died, my life has been weary and
    dreary;   136
Sick at heart have I been, beyond the healing of friendship.
Oft in my lonely hours have I thought of the maiden
    Priscilla.
She is alone in the world; her father and mother and
    brother
Died in the winter together; I saw her going and coming,   140
Now to the grave of the dead, and now to the bed of the
    dying,
Patient, courageous, and strong, and said to myself,
    that if ever

There were angels on earth, as there are angels in heaven,
Two have I seen and known; and the angel whose name is Priscilla
Holds in my desolate life the place which the other abandoned. 145
Long have I cherished the thought, but never have dared to reveal it,
Being a coward in this, though valiant enough for the most part.
Go to the damsel Priscilla, the loveliest maiden of Plymouth,
Say that a blunt old Captain, a man not of words but of actions,
Offers his hand and his heart, the hand and heart of a soldier. 150
Not in these words, you know, but this in short is my meaning;
I am a maker of war, and not a maker of phrases.
You, who are bred as a scholar, can say it in elegant language,
Such as you read in your books of the pleadings and wooings of lovers,
Such as you think best adapted to win the heart of a maiden." 155

When he had spoken, John Alden, the fair-haired, taciturn stripling,
All aghast at his words, surprised, embarrassed, bewildered,
Trying to mask his dismay by treating the subject with lightness,
Trying to smile, and yet feeling his heart stand still in his bosom,
Just as a timepiece stops in a house that is stricken by lightning, 160
Thus made answer and spake, or rather stammered than answered:
"Such a message as that, I am sure I should mangle and mar it;
If you would have it well done, — I am only repeating your maxim, —
You must do it yourself, you must not leave it to others!"
But with the air of a man whom nothing can turn from his purpose, 165
Gravely shaking his head, made answer the Captain of Plymouth:
"Truly the maxim is good, and I do not mean to gainsay it;

But we must use it discreetly, and not waste powder for nothing.
Now, as I said before, I was never a maker of phrases.
I can march up to a fortress and summon the place to surrender, 170
But march up to a woman with such a proposal, I dare not.
I'm not afraid of bullets, nor shot from the mouth of a cannon,
But of a thundering ' No ! ' point-blank from the mouth of a woman,
That I confess I'm afraid of, nor am I ashamed to confess it !
So you must grant my request, for you are an elegant scholar, 175
Having the graces of speech, and skill in the turning of phrases."
Taking the hand of his friend, who still was reluctant and doubtful,
Holding it long in his own, and pressing it kindly, he added:
" Though I have spoken thus lightly, yet deep is the feeling that prompts me;

Surely you cannot refuse what I ask in the name of our friendship!" 180
Then made answer John Alden: "The name of friendship is sacred;
What you demand in that name, I have not the power to deny you!"
So the strong will prevailed, subduing and moulding the gentler,
Friendship prevailed over love, and Alden went on his errand.

III

THE LOVER'S ERRAND

So the strong will prevailed, and Alden went on his errand, 185
Out of the street of the village, and into the paths of the forest,
Into the tranquil woods, where bluebirds and robins were building
Towns in the populous trees, with hanging gardens of verdure,
Peaceful, aerial cities of joy and affection and freedom.

All around him was calm, but within him commotion
  and conflict, 190
Love contending with friendship, and self with each
  generous impulse.
To and fro in his breast his thoughts were heaving and
  dashing,
As in a foundering ship, with every roll of the vessel,
Washes the bitter sea, the merciless surge of the ocean!
"Must I relinquish it all," he cried with a wild lamentation, 195
"Must I relinquish it all, the joy, the hope, the illusion?
Was it for this I have loved, and waited, and worshipped
  in silence?
Was it for this I have followed the flying feet and the
  shadow
Over the wintry sea, to the desolate shores of New England?
Truly the heart is deceitful, and out of its depths of
  corruption 200
Rise, like an exhalation, the misty phantoms of passion;
Angels of light they seem, but are only delusions of
  Satan.
All is clear to me now; I feel it, I see it distinctly!
This is the hand of the Lord; it is laid upon me in anger,

For I have followed too much the heart's desires and
 devices, 205
Worshipping Astaroth blindly, and impious idols of
 Baal.
This is the cross I must bear; the sin and the swift
 retribution."

So through the Plymouth woods John Alden went on
 his errand;
Crossing the brook at the ford, where it brawled over
 pebble and shallow,
Gathering still as he went, the Mayflowers blooming
 around him, 210
Fragrant, filling the air with a strange and wonderful
 sweetness,
Children lost in the woods, and covered with leaves in
 their slumber.
"Puritan flowers," he said, "and the type of Puritan
 maidens,
Modest and simple and sweet, the very type of Priscilla!
So I will take them to her; to Priscilla the Mayflower
 of Plymouth, 215
Modest and simple and sweet, as a parting gift will I
 take them;

Breathing their silent farewells, as they fade and wither and perish,
Soon to be thrown away as is the heart of the giver."
So through the Plymouth woods John Alden went on his errand;
Came to an open space, and saw the disk of the ocean,
Sailless, sombre and cold with the comfortless breath of the east-wind; 221
Saw the new-built house, and people at work in a meadow;
Heard, as he drew near the door, the musical voice of Priscilla
Singing the hundredth Psalm, the grand old Puritan anthem,
Music that Luther sang to the sacred words of the Psalmist, 225
Full of the breath of the Lord, consoling and comforting many.
Then, as he opened the door, he beheld the form of the maiden
Seated beside her wheel, and the carded wool like a snow-drift
Piled at her knee, her white hands feeding the ravenous spindle,

While with her foot on the treadle she guided the wheel in its motion. 230
Open wide on her lap lay the well-worn psalm-book of Ainsworth,
Printed in Amsterdam, the words and the music together,
Rough-hewn, angular notes, like stones in the wall of a churchyard,
Darkened and overhung by the running vine of the verses.
Such was the book from whose pages she sang the old Puritan anthem, 235
She, the Puritan girl, in the solitude of the forest,
Making the humble house and the modest apparel of homespun
Beautiful with her beauty, and rich with the wealth of her being!
Over him rushed, like a wind that is keen and cold and relentless,
Thoughts of what might have been, and the weight and woe of his errand; 240
All the dreams that had faded, and all the hopes that had vanished,
All his life henceforth a dreary and tenantless mansion,

Haunted by vain regrets, and pallid, sorrowful faces.
Still he said to himself, and almost fiercely he said it,
" Let not him that putteth his hand to the plough look backwards; 245
Though the ploughshare cut through the flowers of life to its fountains,
Though it pass o'er the graves of the dead and the hearts of the living,
It is the will of the Lord; and his mercy endureth forever!"

So he entered the house; and the hum of the wheel and the singing
Suddenly ceased; for Priscilla, aroused by his step on the threshold, 250
Rose as he entered and gave him her hand, in signal of welcome,
Saying, "I knew it was you, when I heard your step in the passage;
For I was thinking of you, as I sat there singing and spinning."
Awkward and dumb with delight, that a thought of him had been mingled

Thus in the sacred psalm, that came from the heart of the maiden, 255
Silent before her he stood, and gave her the flowers for an answer,
Finding no words for his thought. He remembered that day in the winter,
After the first great snow, when he broke a path from the village,
Reeling and plunging along through the drifts that encumbered the doorway,
Stamping the snow from his feet as he entered the house, and Priscilla 260
Laughed at his snowy locks, and gave him a seat by the fireside,
Grateful and pleased to know he had thought of her in the snow-storm.
Had he but spoken then! perhaps not in vain had he spoken;
Now it was all too late; the golden moment had vanished!
So he stood there abashed, and gave her the flowers for an answer. 265

Then they sat down and talked of the birds and the beautiful Spring-time;

Talked of their friends at home, and the Mayflower that sailed on the morrow.
"I have been thinking all day," said gently the Puritan maiden,
"Dreaming all night, and thinking all day, of the hedgerows of England, —
They are in blossom now, and the country is all like a garden; 270
Thinking of lanes and fields, and the song of the lark and the linnet,
Seeing the village street, and familiar faces of neighbours
Going about as of old, and stopping to gossip together,
And, at the end of the street, the village church, with the ivy
Climbing the old grey tower, and the quiet graves in the churchyard. 275
Kind are the people I live with, and dear to me my religion;
Still my heart is so sad, that I wish myself back in Old England.
You will say it is wrong, but I cannot help it: I almost
Wish myself back in Old England, I feel so lonely and wretched."

Thereupon answered the youth: "Indeed I do not condemn you; 280
Stouter hearts than a woman's have quailed in this terrible winter.
Yours is tender and trusting, and needs a stronger to lean on;
So I have come to you now, with an offer and proffer of marriage
Made by a good man and true, Miles Standish the Captain of Plymouth!"
Thus he delivered his message, the dexterous writer of letters, — 285
Did not embellish the theme, nor array it in beautiful phrases,
But came straight to the point, and blurted it out like a school-boy;
Even the Captain himself could hardly have said it more bluntly.
Mute with amazement and sorrow, Priscilla the Puritan maiden
Looked into Alden's face, her eyes dilated with wonder, 290
Feeling his words like a blow, that stunned her and rendered her speechless;

Till at length she exclaimed, interrupting the ominous silence:
"If the great Captain of Plymouth is so very eager to wed me,
Why does he not come himself, and take the trouble to woo me?
If I am not worth the wooing, I surely am not worth the winning!" 295
Then John Alden began explaining and smoothing the matter,
Making it worse as he went, by saying the Captain was busy, —
Had no time for such things; — such things! the words grating harshly
Fell on the ear of Priscilla; and swift as a flash she made answer:
"Has he no time for such things, as you call it, before he is married, 300
Would he be likely to find it, or make it, after the wedding?
That is the way with you men; you don't understand us, you cannot.
When you have made up your minds, after thinking of this one and that one,

Choosing, selecting, rejecting, comparing one with
 another,
Then you make known your desire, with abrupt and
 sudden avowal, 305
And are offended and hurt, and indignant perhaps,
 that a woman
Does not respond at once to a love that she never sus-
 pected,
Does not attain at a bound the height to which you
 have been climbing.
This is not right nor just; for surely a woman's affec-
 tion
Is not a thing to be asked for, and had for only the
 asking. 310
When one is truly in love, one not only says it, but
 shows it.
Had he but waited awhile, had he only showed that
 he loved me,
Even this Captain of yours — who knows? — at last
 might have won me,
Old and rough as he is; but now it never can happen."

Still John Alden went on, unheeding the words of
 Priscilla, 315

Urging the suit of his friend, explaining, persuading, expanding;
Spoke of his courage and skill, and of all his battles in Flanders,
How with the people of God he had chosen to suffer affliction,
How, in return for his zeal, they had made him Captain of Plymouth;
He was a gentleman born, could trace his pedigree plainly 320
Back to Hugh Standish of Duxbury Hall, in Lancashire, England,
Who was the son of Ralph, and the grandson of Thurston de Standish;
Heir unto vast estates, of which he was basely defrauded,
Still bore the family arms, and had for his crest a cock argent
Combed and wattled gules, and all the rest of the blazon. 325
He was a man of honor, of noble and generous nature;
Though he was rough, he was kindly; she knew how during the winter
He had attended the sick, with a hand as gentle as woman's;

Somewhat hasty and hot, he could not deny it, and headstrong,
Stern as a soldier might be, but hearty, and placable always,
Not to be laughed at and scorned, because he was little of stature;
For he was great of heart, magnanimous, courtly, courageous;
Any woman in Plymouth, nay, any woman in England,
Might be happy and proud to be called the wife of Miles Standish!

But as he warmed and glowed, in his simple and eloquent language,
Quite forgetful of self, and full of the praise of his rival,
Archly the maiden smiled, and, with eyes overrunning with laughter,
Said, in a tremulous voice, "Why don't you speak for yourself, John?"

IV

JOHN ALDEN

Into the open air John Alden, perplexed and bewildered,

Rushed like a man insane, and wandered alone by the sea-side; 340
Paced up and down the sands, and bared his head to the east-wind,
Cooling his heated brow, and the fire and fever within him.
Slowly, as out of the heavens, with apocalyptical splendors,
Sank the City of God, in the vision of John the Apostle,
So with its cloudy walls of chrysolite, jasper, and sapphire, 345
Sank the broad red sun, and over its turrets uplifted
Glimmered the golden reed of the angel who measured the city.

"Welcome, O wind of the East!" he exclaimed in his wild exultation,
"Welcome, O wind of the East, from the caves of the misty Atlantic!
Blowing o'er fields of dulse, and measureless meadows of sea-grass, 350
Blowing o'er rocky wastes, and the grottoes and gardens of ocean!

Lay thy cold, moist hand on my burning forehead, and wrap me
Close in thy garments of mist, to allay the fever within me!"

Like an awakened conscience, the sea was moaning and tossing,
Beating remorseful and loud the mutable sands of the sea-shore. 355
Fierce in his soul was the struggle and tumult of passions contending;
Love triumphant and crowned, and friendship wounded and bleeding,
Passionate cries of desire, and importunate pleadings of duty!
"Is it my fault," he said, "that the maiden has chosen between us?
Is it my fault that he failed, — my fault that I am the victor?" 360
Then within him there thundered a voice, like the voice of the Prophet:
"It hath displeased the Lord!" — and he thought of David's transgression,
Bathsheba's beautiful face, and his friend in the front of the battle!

Shame and confusion of guilt, and abasement and self-condemnation,
Overwhelmed him at once; and he cried in the deepest contrition: 365
"It hath displeased the Lord! It is the temptation of Satan!"

Then, uplifting his head, he looked at the sea, and beheld there
Dimly the shadowy form of the Mayflower riding at anchor,
Rocked on the rising tide, and ready to sail on the morrow;
Heard the voices of men through the mist, the rattle of cordage 370
Thrown on the deck, the shouts of the mate, and the sailors' "Ay, ay, Sir!"
Clear and distinct, but not loud, in the dripping air of the twilight.
Still for a moment he stood, and listened, and stared at the vessel,
Then went hurriedly on, as one who, seeing a phantom,
Stops, then quickens his pace, and follows the beckoning shadow. 375

"Yes, it is plain to me now," he murmured; "the hand of the Lord is
Leading me out of the land of darkness, the bondage of error,
Through the sea, that shall lift the walls of its waters around me,
Hiding me, cutting me off, from the cruel thoughts that pursue me.
Back will I go o'er the ocean, this dreary land will abandon, 380
Her whom I may not love, and him whom my heart has offended.
Better to be in my grave in the green old churchyard in England,
Close to my mother's side, and among the dust of my kindred;
Better be dead and forgotten, than living in shame and dishonor!
Sacred and safe and unseen, in the dark of the narrow chamber 385
With me my secret shall lie, like a buried jewel that glimmers
Bright on the hand that is dust, in the chambers of silence and darkness, —

Yes, as the marriage ring of the great espousal hereafter!"

Thus as he spake, he turned, in the strength of his strong resolution,
Leaving behind him the shore, and hurried along in the twilight,
Through the congenial gloom of the forest silent and sombre,
Till he beheld the lights in the seven houses of Plymouth,
Shining like seven stars in the dusk and mist of the evening.
Soon he entered his door, and found the redoubtable Captain
Sitting alone, and absorbed in the martial pages of Cæsar,
Fighting some great campaign in Hainault or Brabant or Flanders.
"Long have you been on your errand," he said with a cheery demeanor,
Even as one who is waiting an answer, and fears not the issue.
"Not far off is the house, although the woods are between us;

But you have lingered so long, that while you were going and coming 400
I have fought ten battles and sacked and demolished a city.
Come, sit down, and in order relate to me all that has happened."

Then John Alden spake, and related the wondrous adventure
From beginning to end, minutely, just as it happened;
How he had seen Priscilla, and how he had sped in his courtship, 405
Only smoothing a little, and softening down her refusal.
But when he came at length to the words Priscilla had spoken,
Words so tender and cruel, "Why don't you speak for yourself, John?"
Up leaped the Captain of Plymouth, and stamped on the floor, till his armor
Clanged on the wall, where it hung, with a sound of sinister omen. 410
All his pent-up wrath burst forth in a sudden explosion,

E'en as a hand-grenade, that scatters destruction around it.
Wildly he shouted, and loud: "John Alden! you have betrayed me!
Me, Miles Standish, your friend! have supplanted, defrauded, betrayed me!
One of my ancestors ran his sword through the heart of Wat Tyler; 415
Who shall prevent me from running my own through the heart of a traitor?
Yours is the greater treason, for yours is a treason to friendship!
You, who lived under my roof, whom I cherished and loved as a brother;
You, who have fed at my board, and drunk at my cup, to whose keeping
I have intrusted my honor, my thoughts the most sacred and secret, — 420
You too, Brutus! ah, woe to the name of friendship hereafter!
Brutus was Cæsar's friend, and you were mine, but henceforward
Let there be nothing between us save war, and implacable hatred!"

So spake the Captain of Plymouth, and strode about in the chamber,
Chafing and choking with rage; like cords were the veins on his temples. 425
But in the midst of his anger a man appeared at the doorway,
Bringing in uttermost haste a message of urgent importance.
Rumors of danger and war and hostile incursions of Indians!
Straightway the Captain paused, and, without further question or parley,
Took from the nail on the wall his sword with its scabbard of iron, 430
Buckled the belt round his waist, and, frowning fiercely, departed.
Alden was left alone. He heard the clank of the scabbard
Growing fainter and fainter, and dying away in the distance.
Then he arose from his seat, and looked forth into the darkness,
Felt the cool air blow on his cheek, that was hot with the insult, 435

Lifted his eyes to the heavens, and, folding his hands as in childhood,
Prayed in the silence of night to the Father who seeth in secret.

  Meanwhile the choleric Captain strode wrathful away to the council,
Found it already assembled, impatiently waiting his coming;
Men in the middle of life, austere and grave in deportment,
    440
Only one of them old, the hill that was nearest to heaven,
Covered with snow, but erect, the excellent Elder of Plymouth.°
God had sifted three kingdoms to find the wheat for this planting,
Then had sifted the wheat, as the living seed of a nation;
So say the chronicles old, and such is the faith of the people!
    445
Near them was standing an Indian, in attitude stern and defiant,
Naked down to the waist, and grim and ferocious in aspect;

While on the table before them was lying unopened a Bible,
Ponderous, bound in leather, brass-studded, printed in Holland,
And beside it outstretched the skin of a rattlesnake glittered, 450
Filled, like a quiver, with arrows: a signal and challenge of warfare,
Brought by the Indian, and speaking with arrowy tongues of defiance.
This Miles Standish beheld, as he entered, and heard them debating
What were an answer befitting the hostile message and menace,
Talking of this and of that, contriving, suggesting, objecting; 455
One voice only for peace, and that the voice of the Elder,
Judging it wise and well that some at least were converted,
Rather than any were slain, for this was but Christian behavior!
Then out spake Miles Standish, the stalwart Captain of Plymouth,

Muttering deep in his throat, for his voice was husky with anger, 460

"What! do you mean to make war with milk and the water of roses?

Is it to shoot red squirrels you have your howitzer planted

There on the roof of the church, or is it to shoot red devils?

Truly the only tongue that is understood by a savage

Must be the tongue of fire that speaks from the mouth of the cannon!" 465

Thereupon answered and said the excellent Elder of Plymouth,

Somewhat amazed and alarmed at this irreverent language:

"Not so thought Saint Paul, nor yet the other Apostles;

Not from the cannon's mouth were the tongues of fire they spake with!"

But unheeded fell this mild rebuke on the Captain, 470

Who had advanced to the table, and thus continued discoursing:

"Leave this matter to me, for to me by right it pertaineth.

War is a terrible trade; but in the cause that is righteous,
Sweet is the smell of powder; and thus I answer the challenge!"

Then from the rattlesnake's skin, with a sudden, contemptuous gesture,   475
Jerking the Indian arrows, he filled it with powder and bullets
Full to the very jaws, and handed it back to the savage,
Saying, in thundering tones: "Here, take it! this is your answer!"
Silently out of the room then glided the glistening savage,
Bearing the serpent's skin, and seeming himself like a serpent,   480
Winding his sinuous way in the dark to the depths of the forest.

V

THE SAILING OF THE MAYFLOWER

Just in the grey of the dawn, as the mists uprose from the meadows,

There was a stir and a sound in the slumbering village
  of Plymouth;
Clanging and clicking of arms, and the order imperative, "Forward!"
Given in tone suppressed, a tramp of feet, and then
  silence. 485
Figures ten, in the mist, marched slowly out of the
  village.
Standish the stalwart it was, with eight of his valorous
  army,
Led by their Indian guide, by Hobomok, friend of the
  white men,
Northward marching to quell the sudden revolt of the
  savage.
Giants they seemed in the mist, or the mighty men of
  King David; 490
Giants in heart they were, who believed in God and the
  Bible, —
Ay, who believed in the smiting of Midianites and
  Philistines.
Over them gleamed far off the crimson banners of morning;
Under them loud on the sands, the serried billows, advancing,
Fired along the line, and in regular order retreated. 495

THE COURTSHIP OF MILES STANDISH

Many a mile had they marched, when at length the village of Plymouth
Woke from its sleep, and arose, intent on its manifold labors.
Sweet was the air and soft; and slowly the smoke from the chimneys
Rose over roofs of thatch, and pointed steadily eastward;
Men came forth from the doors, and paused and talked of the weather, 500
Said that the wind had changed, and was blowing fair for the Mayflower;
Talked of their Captain's departure, and all the dangers that menaced,
He being gone, the town, and what should be done in his absence.
Merrily sang the birds, and the tender voices of women
Consecrated with hymns the common cares of the household. 505
Out of the sea rose the sun, and the billows rejoiced at his coming;
Beautiful were his feet on the purple tops of the mountains;
Beautiful on the sails of the Mayflower riding at anchor,

Battered and blackened and worn by all the storms of the winter.
Loosely against her masts was hanging and flapping her canvas, 510
Rent by so many gales, and patched by the hands of the sailors.
Suddenly from her side, as the sun rose over the ocean,
Darted a puff of smoke, and floated seaward; anon rang
Loud over field and forest the cannon's roar, and the echoes
Heard and repeated the sound, the signal-gun of departure! 515
Ah! but with louder echoes replied the hearts of the people!
Meekly, in voices subdued, the chapter was read from the Bible,
Meekly the prayer was begun, but ended in fervent entreaty!
Then from the houses in haste came forth the Pilgrims of Plymouth,
Men and women and children, all hurrying down to the sea-shore, 520
Eager, with tearful eyes, to say farewell to the Mayflower,

Homeward bound o'er the sea, and leaving them here in the desert.

  Foremost among them was Alden. All night he had lain without slumber,
Turning and tossing about in the heat and unrest of his fever.
He had beheld Miles Standish, who came back late from the council, 525
Stalking into the room, and heard him mutter and murmur,
Sometimes it seemed a prayer, and sometimes it sounded like swearing.
Once he had come to the bed, and stood there a moment in silence;
Then he had turned away, and said: "I will not awake him;
Let him sleep on, it is best; for what is the use of more talking!" 530
Then he extinguished the light, and threw himself down on his pallet,
Dressed as he was, and ready to start at the break of the morning, —
Covered himself with the cloak he had worn in his campaigns in Flanders, —

Slept as a soldier sleeps in his bivouac, ready for action.
But with the dawn he arose; in the twilight Alden beheld him 535
Put on his corselet of steel, and all the rest of his armor,
Buckle about his waist his trusty blade of Damascus,
Take from the corner his musket, and so stride out of the chamber.
Often the heart of the youth had burned and yearned to embrace him,
Often his lips had essayed to speak, imploring for pardon, 540
All the old friendship came back with its tender and grateful emotions;
But his pride overmastered the nobler nature within him, —
Pride, and the sense of his wrong, and the burning fire of the insult.
So he beheld his friend departing in anger, but spake not,
Saw him go forth to danger, perhaps to death, and he spake not! 545
Then he arose from his bed, and heard what the people were saying,

Joined in the talk at the door, with Stephen and Richard
    and Gilbert,
Joined in the morning prayer, and in the reading of
    Scripture.
And, with the others, in haste went hurrying down to
    the sea-shore,
Down to the Plymouth Rock, that had been to their
    feet as a doorstep   550
Into a world unknown — the corner-stone of a nation!

There with his boat was the Master, already a little
    impatient
Lest he should lose the tide, or the wind might shift to
    the eastward,
Square-built, hearty, and strong, with an odor of ocean
    about him,
Speaking with this one and that, and cramming letters
    and parcels   555
Into his pockets capacious, and messages mingled to-
    gether
Into his narrow brain, till at last he was wholly bewil-
    dered.
Nearer the boat stood Alden, with one foot placed on
    the gunwale,

One still firm on the rock, and talking at times with sailors,
Seated erect on the thwarts, already and eager for starting. 560
He too was eager to go, and thus put an end to his anguish,
Thinking to fly from despair, that swifter than keel is or canvas,
Thinking to drown in the sea the ghost that would rise and pursue him.
But as he gazed on the crowd, he beheld the form of Priscilla
Standing dejected among them, unconscious of all that was passing. 565
Fixed were her eyes upon his, as if she divined his intention,
Fixed with a look so sad, so reproachful, imploring, and patient,
That with a sudden revulsion his heart recoiled from its purpose,
As from the verge of a crag, where one step more is destruction.
Strange is the heart of man, with its quick, mysterious instincts! 570

Strange is the life of man, and fatal or fated are moments,
Whereupon turn, as on hinges, the gates of the wall adamantine!
"Here I remain!" he exclaimed, as he looked at the heavens above him,
Thanking the Lord whose breath had scattered the mist and the madness,
Wherein, blind and lost, to death he was staggering headlong. 575
"Yonder snow-white cloud, that floats in the ether above me,
Seems like a hand that is pointing and beckoning over the ocean.
There is another hand, that is not so spectral and ghost-like,
Holding me, drawing me back, and clasping mine for protection.
Float, O hand of cloud, and vanish away in the ether!
Roll thyself up like a fist, to threaten and daunt me; I heed not 581
Either your warning or menace, or any omen of evil!
There is no land so sacred, no air so pure and so wholesome,

As is the air she breathes, and the soil that is pressed by her footsteps.
Here for her sake will I stay, and like an invisible presence 585
Hover around her forever, protecting, supporting her weakness;
Yes! as my foot was the first that stepped on this rock at the landing,
So, with the blessing of God, shall it be the last at the leaving!"

Meanwhile the Master alert, but with dignified air and important,
Scanning with watchful eye the tide and the wind and the weather, 590
Walked about on the sands, and the people crowded around him
Saying a few last words, and enforcing his careful remembrance.
Then, taking each by the hand, as if he were grasping a tiller,
Into the boat he sprang, and in haste shoved off to his vessel,
Glad in his heart to get rid of all this worry and flurry, 595

Glad to be gone from a land of sand and sickness and sorrow,
Short allowance of victual, and plenty of nothing but Gospel!
Lost in the sound of the oars was the last farewell of the Pilgrims.
O strong hearts and true! not one went back in the Mayflower!
No, not one looked back, who had set his hand to this ploughing! 600

Soon were heard on board the shouts and songs of the sailors
Heaving the windlass round, and hoisting the ponderous anchor.
Then the yards were braced, and all sails set to the west-wind,
Blowing steady and strong; and the Mayflower sailed from the harbor,
Rounded the point of the Gurnet, and leaving far to the southward 605
Island and cape of sand, and the Field of the First Encounter,
Took the wind on her quarter, and stood for the open Atlantic,

Borne on the sand of the sea, and the swelling hearts of the Pilgrims.

Long in silence they watched the receding sail of the vessel,
Much endeared to them all, as something living and human; 610
Then, as if filled with the spirit, and wrapt in a vision prophetic,
Baring his hoary head, the excellent Elder of Plymouth
Said, " Let us pray ! " and they prayed, and thanked the Lord and took courage.
Mournfully sobbed the waves at the base of the rock, and above them
Bowed and whispered the wheat on the hill of death, and their kindred 615
Seemed to awake in their graves, and to join in the prayer that they uttered.

Sun-illumined and white, on the eastern verge of the ocean
Gleamed the departing sail, like a marble slab in a graveyard;

Buried beneath it lay forever all hope of escaping.
Lo! as they turned to depart, they saw the form of an Indian, 620
Watching them from the hill: but while they spake with each other,
Pointing with outstretched hands, and saying, "Look!" he had vanished.
So they returned to their homes; but Alden lingered a little,
Musing alone on the shore, and watching the wash of the billows
Round the base of the rock, and the sparkle and flash of the sunshine, 625
Like the spirit of God, moving visibly over the waters.

VI

PRISCILLA

Thus for a while he stood, and mused by the shore of the ocean,
Thinking of many things, and most of all of Priscilla;
And as if thought had the power to draw to itself, like the loadstone,

Whatsoever it touches, by subtile laws of its nature, 630
Lo! as he turned to depart, Priscilla was standing beside him.

"Are you so much offended, you will not speak to me?" said she.
"Am I so much to blame, that yesterday, when you were pleading
Warmly the cause of another, my heart, impulsive and wayward,
Pleaded your own, and spake out, forgetful perhaps of decorum? 635
Certainly you can forgive me for speaking so frankly, for saying
What I ought not to have said, yet now I can never unsay it;
For there are moments in life, when the heart is so full of emotion,
That if by chance it be shaken, or into its depths like a pebble
Drops some careless word, it overflows, and its secret, 640
Spilt on the ground like water, can never be gathered together.

THE COURTSHIP OF MILES STANDISH 255

Yesterday I was shocked, when I heard you speak of Miles Standish,
Praising his virtues, transforming his very defects into virtues,
Praising his courage and strength, and even his fighting in Flanders,
As if by fighting alone you could win the heart of a woman, 645
Quite overlooking yourself and the rest, in exalting your hero.
Therefore I spake as I did, by an irresistible impulse.
You will forgive me, I hope, for the sake of the friendship between us,
Which is too true and too sacred to be so easily broken!"
Thereupon answered John Alden, the scholar, the friend of Miles Standish: 650
"I was not angry with you, with myself alone I was angry,
Seeing how badly I managed the matter I had in my keeping."
"No!" interrupted the maiden, with answer prompt and decisive;
"No; you were angry with me, for speaking so frankly and freely.

It was wrong, I acknowledge; for it is the fate of a
  woman 655
Long to be patient and silent, to wait like a ghost that
  is speechless,
Till some questioning voice dissolves the spell of its
  silence.
Hence is the inner life of so many suffering women
Sunless and silent and deep, like subterranean rivers
Running through caverns of darkness, unheard, unseen,
  and unfruitful, 660
Chafing their channels of stone, with endless and profit-
  less murmurs."
Thereupon answered John Alden, the young man, the
  lover of women:
"Heaven forbid it, Priscilla; and truly they seem to me
  always
More like the beautiful rivers that watered the garden
  of Eden,
More like the river Euphrates, through deserts of Havi-
  lah flowing, 665
Filling the land with delight, and memories sweet of the
  garden!"
"Ah, by these words, I can see," again interrupted the
  maiden,

THE COURTSHIP OF MILES STANDISH 257

" How very little you prize me, or care for what I am
    saying.
When from the depths of my heart, in pain and with
    secret misgiving,
Frankly I speak to you, asking for sympathy only and
    kindness,   670
Straightway you take up my words, that are plain and
    direct and in earnest,
Turn them away from their meaning, and answer with
    flattering phrases.
This is not right, is not just, is not true to the best that
    is in you;
For I know and esteem you, and feel that your nature is
    noble,
Lifting mine up to a higher, a more ethereal level.   675
Therefore I value your friendship, and feel it perhaps the
    more keenly
If you say aught that implies I am only as one among
    many,
If you make use of those common and complimentary
    phrases
Most men think so fine, in dealing and speaking with
    women,   679
But which women reject as insipid, if not as insulting."

Mute and amazed was Alden; and listened and looked at Priscilla,
Thinking he never had seen her more fair, more divine in her beauty.
He who but yesterday pleaded so glibly the cause of another,
Stood there embarrassed and silent, and seeking in vain for an answer.
So the maiden went on, and little divined or imagined
What was at work in his heart, that made him so awkward and speechless. 686
"Let us, then, be what we are, and speak what we think, and in all things
Keep ourselves loyal to truth, and the sacred professions of friendship.
It is no secret I tell you, nor am I ashamed to declare it:
I have liked to be with you, to see you, to speak with you always. 690
So I was hurt at your words, and a little affronted to hear you
Urge me to marry your friend, though he were the Captain Miles Standish.
For I must tell you the truth: much more to me is your friendship

Than all the love he could give, were he twice the hero you think him."
Then she extended her hand, and Alden, who eagerly grasped it, 695
Felt all the wounds in his heart, that were aching and bleeding so sorely,
Healed by the touch of that hand, and he said, with a voice full of feeling:
"Yes, we must ever be friends; and of all who offer you friendship
Let me be ever the first, the truest, the nearest and dearest!"

Casting a farewell look at the glimmering sail of the Mayflower 700
Distant, but still in sight, and sinking below the horizon,
Homeward together they walked, with a strange, indefinite feeling,
That all the rest had departed and left them alone in the desert.
But, as they went through the fields in the blessing and smile of the sunshine,
Lighter grew their hearts, and Priscilla said very archly: 705

"Now that our terrible Captain has gone in pursuit of the Indians,
Where he is happier far than he would be commanding a household,
You may speak boldly, and tell me of all that happened between you,
When you returned last night, and said how ungrateful you found me."
Thereupon answered John Alden, and told her the whole of the story, — 710
Told her his own despair, and the direful wrath of Miles Standish.
Whereat the maiden smiled, and said between laughing and earnest,
"He is a little chimney, and heated hot in a moment!"
But as he gently rebuked her, and told her how much he had suffered, —
How he had even determined to sail that day in the Mayflower, 715
And had remained for her sake, on hearing the dangers that threatened, —
All her manner was changed, and she said with a faltering accent,

"Truly I thank you for this: how good you have been
   to me always!"

Thus, as a pilgrim devout, who toward Jerusalem
   journeys,
Taking three steps in advance, and one reluctantly back-
   ward,   720
Urged by importunate zeal, and withheld by pangs of
   contrition;
Slowly but steadily onward, receding yet ever advanc-
   ing,
Journeyed this Puritan youth to the Holy Land of his
   longings,
Urged by the fervor of love, and withheld by remorse-
   ful misgivings.

VII

THE MARCH OF MILES STANDISH

Meanwhile the stalwart Miles Standish was marching
   steadily northward,   725
Winding through forest and swamp, and along the trend
   of the sea-shore,
All day long, with hardly a halt, the fire of his anger

Burning and crackling within, and the sulphurous odour of powder
Seeming more sweet to his nostrils than all the scents of the forest.
Silent and moody he went, and much he revolved his discomfort; 730
He who was used to success, and to easy victories always,
Thus to be flouted, rejected, and laughed to scorn by a maiden,
Thus to be mocked and betrayed by the friend whom most he had trusted!
Ah! 'twas too much to be borne, and he fretted and chafed in his armor!

"I alone am to blame," he muttered, "for mine was the folly. 735
What has a rough old soldier, grown grim and grey in the harness,
Used to the camp and its ways, to do with the wooing of maidens?
'Twas but a dream, — let it pass, — let it vanish like so many others!
What I thought was a flower is only a weed, and is worthless;

THE COURTSHIP OF MILES STANDISH 263

Out of my heart will I pluck it, and throw it away, and henceforward 740
Be but a fighter of battles, a lover and wooer of dangers."
Thus he revolved in his mind his sorry defeat and discomfort,
While he was marching by day or lying at night in the forest,
Looking up at the trees and the constellations beyond them.

After a three days' march he came to an Indian encampment 745
Pitched on the edge of a meadow, between the sea and the forest;
Women at work by the tents, and warriors, horrid with war-paint,
Seated about a fire, and smoking and talking together;
Who, when they saw from afar the sudden approach of the white men,
Saw the flash of the sun on breastplate and sabre and musket, 750
Straightway leaped to their feet, and two, from among them advancing,°

Came to parley with Standish, and offer him furs as a present;
Friendship was in their looks, but in their hearts there was hatred.
Braves of the tribe were these, and brothers, gigantic in stature,
Huge as Goliath of Gath, or the terrible Og, king of Bashan; 755
One was Pecksuot named, and the other was called Wattawamat.
Round their necks were suspended their knives in scabbards of wampum,
Two-edged, trenchant knives, with points as sharp as a needle.
Other arms had they none, for they were cunning and crafty.
"Welcome, English!" they said, — these words they had learned from the traders 760
Touching at times on the coast, to barter and chaffer for peltries.
Then in their native tongue they began to parley with Standish,
Through his guide and interpreter, Hobomok, friend of the white man,

THE COURTSHIP OF MILES STANDISH

Begging for blankets and knives, but mostly for muskets and powder,
Kept by the white man, they said, concealed, with the plague, in his cellars,
Ready to be let loose, and destroy his brother the red man!
But when Standish refused, and said he would give them the Bible,
Suddenly changing their tone, they began to boast and to bluster.
Then Wattawamat advanced with a stride in front of the other,
And, with a lofty demeanor, thus vauntingly spake to the Captain:
"Now Wattawamat can see, by the fiery eyes of the Captain,
Angry is he in his heart; but the heart of the brave Wattawamat
Is not afraid at the sight. He was not born of a woman,
But on a mountain, at night, from an oak-tree riven by lightning,
Forth he sprang at a bound, with all his weapons about him,

Shouting, 'Who is there here to fight with the brave
    Wattawamat?'"
Then he unsheathed his knife, and, whetting the blade
    on his left hand,
Held it aloft and displayed a woman's face on the
    handle,
Saying, with bitter expression and look of sinister
    meaning:
"I have another at home, with the face of a man on the
    handle;   780
By and by they shall marry; and there will be plenty
    of children!"

  Then stood Pecksuot forth, self-vaunting, insulting
    Miles Standish;
While with his fingers he patted the knife that hung
    at his bosom,
Drawing it half from its sheath, and plunging it back,
    as he muttered,
"By and by it shall see; it shall eat; ah, ha! but
    shall speak not!   785
This is the mighty Captain the white men have sent to
    destroy us!
He is a little man; let him go and work with the
    women!"

Meanwhile Standish had noted the faces and figures
  of Indians
Peeping and creeping about from bush to tree in the
  forest,
Feigning to look for game, with arrows set on their
  bow-strings, 790
Drawing about him still closer and closer the net of
  their ambush.
But undaunted he stood, and dissembled and treated
  them smoothly;
So the old chronicles say, that were writ in the days
  of the fathers.
But when he heard their defiance, the boast, the taunt
  and the insult,
All the hot blood of his race, of Sir Hugh and of Thurs-
  ton de Standish, 795
Boiled and beat in his heart, and swelled in the veins
  of his temples.
Headlong he leaped on the boaster, and, snatching his
  knife from its scabbard,
Plunged it into his heart, and, reeling backward, the
  savage
Fell with his face to the sky, and a fiendlike fierceness
  upon it.

Straight there arose from the forest the awful sound of the war-whoop, 800
And, like a flurry of snow on the whistling wind of December,
Swift and sudden and keen came a flight of feathery arrows.
Then came a cloud of smoke, and out of the cloud came the lightning,
Out of the lightning thunder; and death unseen ran before it.
Frightened the savages fled for shelter in swamp and in thicket, 805
Hotly pursued and beset; but their sachem, the brave Wattawamat,
Fled not; he was dead. Unswerving and swift had a bullet
Passed through his brain, and he fell with both hands clutching the greensward,
Seeming in death to hold back from his foe the land of his fathers.

There on the flowers of the meadow the warriors lay, and above them, 810
Silent, with folded arms, stood Hobomok, friend of the white man.

Smiling at length he exclaimed to the stalwart Captain of Plymouth:
"Pecksuot bragged very loud, of his courage, his strength and his stature, —
Mocked the great Captain, and called him a little man; but I see now
Big enough have you been to lay him speechless before you!" 815

Thus the first battle was fought and won by the stalwart Miles Standish.
When the tidings thereof were brought to the village of Plymouth,
And as a trophy of war the head of the brave Wattawamat
Scowled from the roof of the fort, which at once was a church and a fortress,
All who beheld it rejoiced, and praised the Lord, and took courage 820
Only Priscilla averted her face from this spectre of terror,
Thanking God in her heart that she had not married Miles Standish;
Shrinking, fearing almost, lest, coming home from his battles,

He should lay claim to her hand, as the prize and reward of his valor.

VIII

THE SPINNING WHEEL

Month after month passed away, and in autumn the ships of the merchants 825
Came with kindred and friends, with cattle and corn for the Pilgrims.
All in the village was peace; the men were intent on their labors,
Busy with hewing and building, with garden-plot and with merestead,
Busy with breaking the glebe, and mowing the grass in the meadows,
Searching the sea for its fish, and hunting the deer in the forest. 830
All in the village was peace; but at times the rumor of warfare
Filled the air with alarm, and the apprehension of danger.
Bravely the stalwart Standish was scouring the land with his forces,

Waxing valiant in fight and defeating the alien armies,
Till his name had become a sound of fear to the nations. 835
Anger was still in his heart, but at times the remorse and contrition
Which in all noble natures succeed the passionate outbreak,
Came like a rising tide, that encounters the rush of a river,
Staying its current awhile, but making it bitter and brackish.

Meanwhile Alden at home had built him a new habitation, 840
Solid, substantial, of timber rough-hewn from the firs of the forest.
Wooden-barred was the door, and the roof was covered with rushes;
Latticed the windows were, and the window-panes were of paper,
Oiled to admit the light, while wind and rain were excluded.
There too he dug a well, and around it planted an orchard: 845

Still may be seen to this day some trace of the well and the orchard.
Close to the house was the stall, where, safe and secure from annoyance,
Raghorn, the snow-white bull, that had fallen to Alden's allotment
In the division of cattle, might ruminate in the nighttime
Over the pastures he cropped, made fragrant by sweet pennyroyal. 850

Oft when his labor was finished, with eager feet would the dreamer
Follow the pathway that ran through the woods to the house of Priscilla,
Led by illusions romantic and subtile deceptions of fancy,
Pleasure disguised as duty, and love in the semblance of friendship.
Ever of her he thought, when he fashioned the walls of his dwelling; 855
Ever of her he thought, when he delved in the soil of his garden;
Ever of her he thought, when he read in his Bible on Sunday

Praise of the virtuous woman, as she is described in
   the Proverbs, —
How the heart of her husband doth safely trust in her
   always,
How all the days of her life she will do him good, and
   not evil, 860
How she seeketh the wool and the flax and worketh
   with gladness,
How she layeth her hand to the spindle and holdeth
   the distaff,
How she is not afraid of the snow for herself or her
   household,
Knowing her household are clothed with the scarlet
   cloth of her weaving!

So as she sat at her wheel one afternoon in the
   Autumn, 865
Alden, who opposite sat, and was watching her dexter-
   ous fingers,
As if the thread she was spinning were that of his life
   and his fortune,
After a pause in their talk, thus spake to the sound of
   the spindle.
"Truly, Priscilla," he said, "when I see you spinning
   and spinning,

Never idle a moment, but thrifty and thoughtful of
others, 870
Suddenly you are transformed, are visibly changed in
a moment;
You are no longer Priscilla, but Bertha the Beautiful
Spinner."
Here the light foot on the treadle grew swifter and
swifter; the spindle
Uttered an angry snarl, and the thread snapped short
in her fingers;
While the impetuous speaker, not heeding the mischief,
continued: 875
"You are the beautiful Bertha, the spinner, the queen
of Helvetia;
She whose story I read at a stall in the streets of
Southampton,
Who, as she rode on her palfrey, o'er valley and meadow
and mountain,
Ever was spinning her thread from a distaff fixed to
her saddle.
She was so thrifty and good, that her name passed
into a proverb. 880
So shall it be with your own, when the spinning-wheel
shall no longer

Hum in the house of the farmer, and fill its chambers with music.
Then shall the mothers, reproving, relate how it was in their childhood,
Praising the good old times, and the days of Priscilla the spinner!"
Straight uprose from her wheel the beautiful Puritan maiden, 885
Pleased with the praise of her thrift from him whose praise was the sweetest,
Drew from the reel on the table a snowy skein of her spinning,
Thus making answer, meanwhile, to the flattering phrases of Alden:
"Come, you must not be idle; if I am a pattern for housewives,
Show yourself equally worthy of being the model of husbands. 890
Hold this skein on your hands, while I wind it, ready for knitting;
Then who knows but hereafter, when fashions have changed and the manners,
Fathers may talk to their sons of the good old times of John Alden!"

Thus, with a jest and a laugh, the skein on his hands she adjusted,
He sitting awkwardly there, with his arms extended before him, 895
She standing graceful, erect, and winding the thread from his fingers,
Sometimes chiding a little his clumsy manner of holding,
Sometimes touching his hands, as she disentangled expertly
Twist or knot in the yarn, unawares — for how could she help it? —
Sending electrical thrills through every nerve in his body. 900

Lo! in the midst of this scene, a breathless messenger entered,
Bringing in hurry and heat the terrible news from the village.
Yes; Miles Standish was dead! — an Indian had brought them the tidings, —
Slain by a poisoned arrow, shot down in the front of the battle,
Into an ambush beguiled, cut off with the whole of his forces; 905

All the town would be burned, and all the people be murdered!
Such were the tidings of evil that burst on the hearts of the hearers.
Silent and statue-like stood Priscilla, her face looking backward
Still at the face of the speaker, her arms uplifted in horror;
But John Alden, upstarting, as if the barb of the arrow 910
Piercing the heart of his friend had struck his own, and had sundered
Once and forever the bonds that held him bound as a captive,
Wild with excess of sensation, the awful delight of his freedom,
Mingled with pain and regret, unconscious of what he was doing,
Clasped, almost with a groan, the motionless form of Priscilla, 915
Pressing her close to his heart, as forever his own, and exclaiming:
"Those whom the Lord hath united, let no man put them asunder!"

Even as rivulets twain, from distant and separate sources,
Seeing each other afar, as they leap from the rocks, and pursuing
Each one its devious path, but drawing nearer and nearer, 920
Rush together at last, at their trysting-place in the forest;
So these lives that had run thus far in separate channels,
Coming in sight of each other, then swerving and flowing asunder,
Parted by barriers strong, but drawing nearer and nearer, 924
Rushed together at last, and one was lost in the other.

IX

THE WEDDING-DAY

Forth from the curtain of clouds, from the tent of purple and scarlet,
Issued the sun, the great High-Priest, in his garments resplendent,
Holiness unto the Lord, in letters of light, on his forehead,

Round the hem of his robe the golden bells and pomegranates.
Blessing the world he came, and the bars of vapor beneath him 930
Gleamed like a grate of brass, and the sea at his feet was a laver!

This was the wedding morn of Priscilla the Puritan maiden.
Friends were assembled together; the Elder and Magistrate also
Graced the scene with their presence, and stood like the Law and the Gospel,
One with the sanction of earth and one with the blessing of heaven. 935
Simple and brief was the wedding, as that of Ruth and of Boaz.
Softly the youth and the maiden repeated the words of betrothal,
Taking each other for husband and wife in the Magistrate's presence,
After the Puritan way, and the laudable custom of Holland.
Fervently then and devoutly, the excellent Elder of Plymouth 940

Prayed for the hearth and the home, that were founded that day in affection,
Speaking of life and of death, and imploring Divine benedictions.

Lo! when the service was ended, a form appeared on the threshold,
Clad in armor of steel, a sombre and sorrowful figure!
Why does the bridegroom start and stare at the strange apparition? 945
Why does the bride turn pale, and hide her face on his shoulder?
Is it a phantom of air, — a bodiless, spectral illusion?
Is it a ghost from the grave, that has come to forbid the betrothal?
Long had it stood there unseen, a guest uninvited, unwelcomed;
Over its clouded eyes there had passed at times an expression 950
Softening the gloom and revealing the warm heart hidden beneath them,
As when across the sky the driving rack of the rain cloud

Grows for a moment thin, and betrays the sun by its
  brightness.
Once it had lifted its hand, and moved its lips, but
  was silent,
As if an iron will had mastered the fleeting inten-
   tion.   955
But when were ended the troth and the prayer and
  the last benediction,
Into the room it strode, and the people beheld with
  amazement
Bodily there in his armor Miles Standish, the Captain
  of Plymouth!
Grasping the bridegroom's hand, he said with emotion,
  "Forgive me!
I have been angry and hurt, — too long have I cherished
  the feeling;   960
I have been cruel and hard, but now, thank God! it
  is ended.
Mine is the same hot blood that leaped in the veins of
  Hugh Standish,
Sensitive, swift to resent, but as swift in atoning for
  error.
Never so much as now was Miles Standish the friend of
  John Alden."

Thereupon answered the bridegroom: "Let all be forgotten between us, — 965
All save the dear old friendship, and that shall grow older and dearer!"
Then the Captain advanced, and, bowing, saluted Priscilla,
Gravely, and after the manner of old-fashioned gentry in England,
Something of camp and of court, of town and of country, commingled,
Wishing her joy of her wedding, and loudly lauding her husband. 970
Then he said with a smile: "I should have remembered the adage, —
If you will be well served, you must serve yourself; and moreover,
No man can gather cherries in Kent at the season of Christmas!"

Great was the people's amazement, and greater yet their rejoicing,
Thus to behold once more the sunburnt face of their Captain, 975
Whom they had mourned as dead; and they gathered and crowded about him,

Eager to see him and hear him, forgetful of bride and of bridegroom,
Questioning, answering, laughing, and each interrupting the other,
Till the good Captain declared, being quite overpowered and bewildered,
He had rather by far break into an Indian encampment, 980
Than come again to a wedding to which he had not been invited.

Meanwhile the bridegroom went forth and stood with the bride at the doorway,
Breathing the perfumed air of that warm and beautiful morning.
Touched with autumnal tints, but lonely and sad in the sunshine,
Lay extended before them the land of toil and privation; 985
There were the graves of the dead, and the barren waste of the sea-shore,
There the familiar fields, the groves of pine, and the meadows;
But to their eyes transfigured, it seemed as the Garden of Eden,

Filled with the presence of God, whose voice was the sound of the ocean.

Soon was their vision disturbed by the noise and stir of departure, 990
Friends coming forth from the house, and impatient of longer delaying,
Each with his plan for the day, and the work that was left uncompleted.
Then from a stall near at hand, amid exclamations of wonder,
Alden the thoughtful, the careful, so happy, so proud of Priscilla,
Brought out his snow-white bull, obeying the hand of its master, 995
Led by a cord that was tied to an iron ring in its nostrils,
Covered with crimson cloth, and a cushion placed for a saddle.
She should not walk, he said, through the dust and heat of the noonday;
Nay, she should ride like a queen, not plod along like a peasant.
Somewhat alarmed at first, but reassured by the others, 1000

THE COURTSHIP OF MILES STANDISH

Placing her hand on the cushion, her foot in the hand
  of her husband,
Gayly, with joyous laugh, Priscilla mounted her palfrey.
"Nothing is wanting now," he said with a smile, "but
  the distaff;
Then you would be in truth my queen, my beautiful
  Bertha!"

Onward the bridal procession now moved to their
  new habitation,   1005
Happy husband and wife,° and friends conversing to-
  gether.
Pleasantly murmured the brook, as they crossed the
  ford in the forest,
Pleased with the image that passed, like a dream of
  love through its bosom,
Tremulous, floating in air, o'er the depths of the azure
  abysses.
Down through the golden leaves the sun was pouring
  his splendors,   1010
Gleaming on purple grapes, that, from branches above
  them suspended,
Mingled their odorous breath with the balm of the
  pine and the fir tree.

Wild and sweet as the clusters that grew in the valley of Eshcol.
Like a picture it seemed of the primitive, pastoral ages,
Fresh with the youth of the world, and recalling Rebecca and Isaac, 1015
Old and yet ever new, and simple and beautiful always,
Love immortal and young in the endless succession of lovers.
So through the Plymouth woods passed onward the bridal procession.

SNOW-BOUND

A WINTER IDYL

TO THE MEMORY OF

THE HOUSEHOLD IT DESCRIBES

This Poem is Dedicated by the Author

"As the Spirits of Darkness be stronger in the dark, so Good Spirits which be Angels of Light are augmented not only by the Divine light of the Sun, but also by our common VVood Fire: and as the Celestial Fire drives away dark spirits, so also this our Fire of VVood doth the same."— COR. AGRIPPA, *Occult Philosophy*, Book I., ch. v.

> "Announced by all the trumpets of the sky,
> Arrives the snow; and, driving o'er the fields,
> Seems nowhere to alight; the whited air
> Hides hills and woods, the river and the heaven,
> And veils the farm-house at the garden's end.
> The sled and traveller stopped, the courier's feet
> Delayed, all friends shut out, the house-mates sit
> Around the radiant fireplace, inclosed
> In a tumultuous privacy of storm." — EMERSON.

THE sun that brief December day
Rose cheerless over hills of grey,

And, darkly circled, gave at noon
A sadder light than waning moon.
Slow tracing down the thickening sky 5
Its mute and ominous prophecy,
A portent seeming less than threat,
It sank from sight before it set.
A chill no coat, however stout,
Of homespun stuff could quite shut out, 10
A hard, dull bitterness of cold,
   That checked, mid-vein, the circling race
   Of life-blood in the sharpened face,
The coming of the snow-storm told.
The wind blew east; we heard the roar 15
Of Ocean on his wintry shore,
And felt the strong pulse throbbing there
Beat with low rhythm our inland air.

Meanwhile we did our nightly chores, —
Brought in the wood from out of doors, 20
Littered the stalls, and from the mows
Raked down the herd's-grass for the cows:
Heard the horse whinnying for his corn;
And, sharply clashing horn on horn,
Impatient down the stanchion rows 25

The cattle shake their walnut bows;
While, peering from his early perch
Upon the scaffold's pole of birch,
The cock his crested helmet bent
And down his querulous challenge sent.   30
Unwarmed by any sunset light
The grey day darkened into night,
A night made hoary with the swarm
And whirl-dance of the blinding storm,
As zigzag wavering to and fro   35
Crossed and recrossed the wingèd snow:
And ere the early bed-time came
The white drift piled the window-frame,
And through the glass the clothes-line posts
Looked in like tall and sheeted ghosts.   40
So all night long the storm roared on:
The morning broke without a sun;
In tiny spherule traced with lines
Of Nature's geometric signs,
In starry flake, and pellicle,   45
All day the hoary meteor fell;
And, when the second morning shone,
We looked upon a world unknown,
On nothing we could call our own.

Around the glistening wonder bent 50
The blue walls of the firmament,
No cloud above, no earth below, —
A universe of sky and snow!
The old familiar sights of ours
Took marvellous shapes; strange domes and towers 55
Rose up where sty or corn-crib stood,
Or garden wall, or belt of wood;
A smooth white mound the brush-pile showed,
A fenceless drift what once was road;
The bridle-post an old man sat 60
With loose-flung coat and high cocked hat;
The well-curb had a Chinese roof;
And even the long sweep, high aloof,
In its slant splendor seemed to tell
Of Pisa's leaning miracle.° 65

A prompt, decisive man, no breath
Our father wasted: "Boys, a path!"
Well pleased (for when did farmer boy
Count such a summons less than joy?)
Our buskins on our feet we drew; 70
  With mittened hands, and caps drawn low,
  To guard our necks and ears from snow,

We cut the solid whiteness through.
And, where the drift was deepest, made
A tunnel walled and overlaid
With dazzling crystal: we had read
Of rare Aladdin's wondrous cave,
And to our own his name we gave,
With many a wish the luck were ours
To test his lamp's supernal powers.
We reached the barn with merry din,
And roused the prisoned brutes within.
The old horse thrust his long head out,
And grave with wonder gazed about;
The cock his lusty greeting said,
And forth his speckled harem led;
The oxen lashed their tails, and hooked,
And mild reproach of hunger looked;
The hornèd patriarch of the sheep,
Like Egypt's Amun° roused from sleep,
Shook his sage head with gesture mute,
And emphasized with stamp of foot.

All day the gusty north-wind bore
The loosening drift its breath before;
Low circling round its southern zone,

The sun through dazzling snow-mist shone.
No church-bell lent its Christian tone
To the savage air, no social smoke
Curled over woods of snow-hung oak.
A solitude made more intense   100
By dreary-voicèd elements,
The shrieking of the mindless wind,
The moaning tree-boughs swaying blind,
And on the grass the unmeaning beat
Of ghostly finger-tips of sleet.   105
Beyond the circle of our hearth
No welcome sound of toil or mirth
Unbound the spell, and testified
Of human life and thought outside.
We minded that the sharpest ear   110
The buried brooklet could not hear,
The music of whose liquid lip
Had been to us companionship,
And, in our lonely life, had grown
To have an almost human tone.   115

As night drew on, and, from the crest
Of wooded knolls that ridged the west,
The sun, a snow-blown traveller, sank

From sight beneath the smothering bank,
We piled, with care, our nightly stack
Of wood against the chimney-back, —
The oaken log, green, huge, and thick,
And on its top the stout back-stick;
The knotty forestick laid apart,
And filled between with curious art
The ragged brush; then, hovering near,
We watched the first red blaze appear,
Heard the sharp crackle, caught the gleam
On whitewashed wall and sagging beam,
Until the old, rude-furnished room
Burst, flower-like, into rosy bloom;
While radiant with a mimic flame
Outside the sparkling drift became,
And through the bare-boughed lilac-tree
Our own warm hearth seemed blazing free.
The crane and pendent trammels showed,
The Turks' heads on the andirons glowed;
While childish fancy, prompt to tell
The meaning of the miracle,
Whispered the old rhyme: "*Under the tree,*
When fire outdoors burns merrily,
There the witches are making tea."

The moon above the eastern wood
Shone at its full; the hill-range stood
Transfigured in the silver flood, 145
Its blown snows flashing cold and keen,
Dead white, save where some sharp ravine
Took shadow, or the sombre green
Of hemlocks turned to pitchy black
Against the whiteness at their back. 150
For such a world and such a night
Most fitting that unwarming light,
Which only seemed where'er it fell
To make the coldness visible.

Shut in from all the world without, 155
We sat the clean-winged hearth about,
Content to let the north-wind roar
In baffled rage at pane and door,
While the red logs before us beat
The frost-line back with tropic heat; 160
And ever, when a louder blast
Shook beam and rafter as it passed,
The merrier up its roaring draught
The great throat of the chimney laughed;
The house-dog on his paws outspread, 165

Laid to the fire his drowsy head,
The cat's dark silhouette on the wall
A couchant tiger's seemed to fall;
And, for the winter fireside meet,
Between the andirons' straddling feet, 170
The mug of cider simmered slow,
The apples sputtered in a row,
And, close at hand, the basket stood
With nuts from brown October's wood.

What matter how the night behaved? 175
What matter how the north-wind raved?
Blow high, blow low, not all its snow
Could quench our hearth-fire's ruddy glow.
O Time and Change! — with hair as grey
As was my sire's that winter day, 180
How strange it seems, with so much gone
Of life and love, to still live on!
Ah, brother! only I and thou
Are left of all that circle now, —
The dear home faces whereupon 185
That fitful firelight paled and shone.
Henceforward, listen as we will,
The voices of that hearth are still;

Look where we may, the wide earth o'er,
Those lighted faces smile no more.
We tread the paths their feet have worn,
   We sit beneath their orchard trees,
   We hear, like them, the hum of bees,
And rustle of the bladed corn;
We turn the pages that they read,
   Their written words we linger o'er,
But in the sun they cast no shade,
No voice is heard, no sign is made,
   No step is on the conscious floor!
Yet Love will dream, and Faith will trust
(Since He who knows our need is just),
That somehow, somewhere, meet we must.
Alas for him who never sees
The stars shine through his cypress-trees!
Who, hopeless, lays his dead away,
Nor looks to see the breaking day
Across the mournful marbles play!
Who hath not learned, in hours of faith,
   The truth to flesh and sense unknown,
That Life is ever lord of Death,
   And Love can never lose its own!

We sped the time with stories old,
Wrought puzzles out, and riddles told,
Or stammered from our school-book lore
" The Chief of Gambia's° golden shore."   215
How often since, when all the land
Was clay in Slavery's shaping hand,
As if a trumpet called, I've heard
Dame Mercy Warren's rousing word:
" *Does not the voice of reason cry,*   220
   Claim the first right which Nature gave,
From the red scourge of bondage fly,
   Nor deign to live a burdened slave! "
Our father rode again his ride
On Memphremagog's wooded side;   225
Sat down again to moose and samp
In trapper's hut and Indian camp;
Lived o'er the old idyllic ease
Beneath St. François' hemlock trees;
Again for him the moonlight shone   230
On Norman cap and bodiced zone;
Again he heard the violin play
Which led the village dance away,
And mingled in its merry whirl
The grandam and the laughing girl.   235

Or, nearer home, our steps he led
Where Salisbury's level marshes spread
   Mile-wide as flies the laden bee;
Where merry mowers, hale and strong,
Swept, scythe on scythe, their swaths along   240
   The low green prairies of the sea.
We shared the fishing off Boar's Head,
   And round the rocky Isles of Shoals
   The hake-broil on the drift-wood coals;
The chowder on the sand-beach made,   245
Dipped by the hungry, steaming hot,
With spoons of clam-shell from the pot.
We heard the tales of witchcraft old,
And dream and sign and marvel told
To sleepy listeners as they lay   250
Stretched idly on the salted hay,
Adrift along the winding shores,
When favoring breezes deigned to blow
The square sail of the gundelow,
And idle lay the useless oars.   255

Our mother, while she turned her wheel
Or run the new-knit stocking-heel,
Told how the Indian hordes came down

At midnight on Cochecho° town,
And how her own great-uncle bore
His cruel scalp-mark to fourscore.
Recalling, in her fitting phrase,
So rich and picturesque and free,
(The common unrhymed poetry
Of simple life and country ways),
The story of her early days, —
She made us welcome to her home;
Old hearths grew wide to give us room;
We stole with her a frightened look
At the grey wizard's conjuring-book,
The fame whereof went far and wide
Through all the simple country-side;
We heard the hawks at twilight play,
The boat-horn on Piscataqua,
The loon's weird laughter far away;
We fished her little trout-brook, knew
What flowers in wood and meadow grew,
What sunny hillsides autumn-brown
She climbed to shake the ripe nuts down,
Saw where in sheltered cove and bay
The ducks' black squadron anchored lay,
And heard the wild-geese calling loud

Beneath the grey November cloud.
Then, haply, with a look more grave,
And soberer tone, some tale she gave 285
From painful Sewel's ancient tome,°
Beloved in every Quaker home,
Of faith fire-winged by martyrdom,
Or Chalkley's Journal,° old and quaint, —
Gentlest of skippers, rare sea-saint! — 290
Who, when the dreary calms prevailed,
And water-butt and bread-cask failed,
And cruel, hungry eyes pursued
His portly presence mad for food,
With dark hints muttered under breath 295
Of casting lots for life or death,
Offered, if Heaven withheld supplies,
To be himself the sacrifice.
Then, suddenly, as if to save
The good man from his living grave, 300
A ripple on the water grew,
A school of porpoise dashed in view.
"Take, eat," he said, "and be content;
These fishes in my stead are sent
By Him who gave the tangled ram° 305
To spare the child of Abraham."

SNOW-BOUND

Our uncle, innocent of books,
Was rich in lore of fields and brooks,
The ancient teachers never dumb
Of Nature's unhoused lyceum.
In moons and tides and weather wise,
He read the clouds as prophecies,
And foul or fair could well divine,
By many an occult hint and sign,
Holding the cunning-warded keys
To all the woodcraft mysteries;
Himself to Nature's heart so near
That all her voices in his ear
Of beast or bird had meanings clear,
Like Apollonius° of old,
Who knew the tales the sparrows told,
Or Hermes, who interpreted
What the sage cranes of Nilus said;
A simple, guileless, childlike man,
Content to live where life began;
Strong only on his native grounds,
The little world of sights and sounds
Whose girdle was the parish bounds,
Whereof his fondly partial pride
The common features magnified,

As Surrey hills to mountains grew
In White of Selborne's° loving view, —
He told how teal and loon he shot,
And how the eagle's eggs he got,
The feats on pond and river done,   335
The prodigies of rod and gun;
Till, warming with the tales he told,
Forgotten was the outside cold,
The bitter wind unheeded blew:
From ripening corn the pigeons flew,   340
The partridge drummed i' the wood, the mink
Went fishing down the river-brink.
In fields with bean or clover gay,
The woodchuck, like a hermit grey,
Peered from the doorway of his cell;   345
The muskrat plied the mason's trade,
And tier by tier his mud-walls laid;
And from the shagbark overhead
The grizzled squirrel dropped his shell.

Next, the dear aunt, whose smile of cheer   350
And voice in dreams I see and hear, —
The sweetest woman ever Fate
Perverse denied a household mate,

Who, lonely, homeless, not the less
Found peace in love's unselfishness, 355
And welcome wheresoe'er she went,
A calm and gracious element,
Whose presence seemed the sweet income
And womanly atmosphere of home, —
Called up her girlhood memories, 360
The huskings and the apple-bees,
The sleigh-rides and the summer sails,
Weaving through all the poor details
And homespun warp of circumstance
A golden woof-thread of romance. 365
For well she kept her genial mood
And simple faith of maidenhood;
Before her still a cloud-land lay,
The mirage loomed across her way;
The morning dew, that dries so soon 370
With others, glistened at her noon;
Through years of toil and soil and care,
From glossy tress to thin grey hair,
All unprofaned she held apart
The virgin fancies of the heart. 375
Be shame to him of woman born
Who hath for such but thought of scorn.

There, too, our elder sister plied
Her evening task the stand beside;
A full, rich nature, free to trust, 380
Truthful and almost sternly just,
Impulsive, earnest, prompt to act,
And make her generous thought a fact,
Keeping with many a light disguise
The secret of self-sacrifice. 385
O heart sore-tried! thou hast the best
That Heaven itself could give thee, — rest,
Rest from all bitter thoughts and things!
   How many a poor one's blessing went
   With thee beneath the low green tent 390
Whose curtain never outward swings!
As one who held herself a part
Of all she saw, and let her heart
   Against the household bosom lean,
Upon the motley-braided mat 395
Our youngest and our dearest sat,
Lifting her large, sweet, asking eyes,
   Now bathed within the fadeless green°
And holy peace of Paradise.
Oh, looking from some heavenly hill, 400
   Or from the shade of saintly palms,

Or silver reach of river calms,
Do those large eyes behold me still?
With me one little year ago: —
The chill weight of the winter snow
  For months upon her grave has lain;
And now, when summer south-winds blow
  And brier and harebell bloom again,
I tread the pleasant paths we trod,
I see the violet-sprinkled sod
Whereon she leaned, too frail and weak —
The hillside flowers she loved to seek —
Yet following me where'er I went
With dark eyes full of love's content.
The birds are glad; the brier-rose fills
The air with sweetness; all the hills
Stretch green to June's unclouded sky;
But still I wait with ear and eye
For something gone which should be nigh,
A loss in all familiar things,
In flower that blooms, and bird that sings.
And yet, dear heart! remembering thee,
  Am I not richer than of old?
Safe in thy immortality,
  What change can reach the wealth I hold?

   x

What chance can mar the pearl and gold
Thy love hath left in trust with me?
And while in life's late afternoon,
　　Where cool and long the shadows grow,
I walk to meet the night that soon
　　Shall shape and shadow overflow,
I cannot feel that thou art far,
Since near at need the angels are;
And when the sunset gates unbar,
　　Shall I not see thee waiting stand,
And, white against the evening star,
　　The welcome of thy beckoning hand?

Brisk wielder of the birch and rule,
The master of the district school
Held at the fire his favored place;
Its warm glow lit a laughing face
Fresh-hued and fair, where scarce appeared
The uncertain prophecy of beard.
He teased the mitten-blinded cat,
Played cross-pins on my uncle's hat,
Sang songs, and told us what befalls
In classic Dartmouth's college halls.
Born the wild Northern hills among,

From whence his yeoman father wrung
By patient toil subsistence scant,
Not competence and yet not want,
He early gained the power to pay
His cheerful, self-reliant way;
Could doff at ease his scholar's gown
To peddle wares from town to town;
Or through the long vacation's reach
In lonely lowland districts teach,
Where all the droll experience found
At stranger hearths in boarding round,
The moonlit skater's keen delight,
The sleigh-drive through the frosty night,
The rustic party, with its rough
Accompaniment of blind-man's-buff,
And whirling plate, and forfeits paid,
His winter task a pastime made.
Happy the snow-locked homes wherein
He tuned his merry violin,
Or played the athlete in the barn,
Or held the good dame's winding yarn,
Or mirth-provoking versions told
Of classic legends rare and old,
Wherein the scenes of Greece and Rome

Had all the commonplace of home,
And little seemed at best the odds
'Twixt Yankee pedlers and old gods; 475
Where Pindus-born Araxes° took
The guise of any grist-mill brook,
And dread Olympus at his will
Became a huckleberry hill.

A careless boy that night he seemed; 480
  But at his desk he had the look
And air of one who wisely schemed,
  And hostage from the future took
    In trainèd thought and lore of book.
Large-brained, clear-eyed, — of such as he 485
Shall Freedom's young apostles be,
Who, following in War's bloody trail,
Shall every lingering wrong assail;
All chains from limb and spirit strike,
Uplift the black and white alike; 490
Scatter before their swift advance
The darkness and the ignorance,
The pride, the lust, the squalid sloth,
Which nurtured Treason's monstrous growth,
Made murder pastime, and the hell 495

Of prison-torture possible;
The cruel lie of caste refute,
Old forms remould, and substitute
For Slavery's lash the freeman's will,
For blind routine, wise-handed skill;   500
A school-house plant on every hill,
Stretching in radiate nerve-lines thence
The quick wires of intelligence;
Till North and South together brought
Shall own the same electric thought,   505
In peace a common flag salute,
And, side by side in labor's free
And unresentful rivalry,
Harvest the fields wherein they fought.

Another guest° that winter night   510
Flashed back from lustrous eyes the light.
Unmarked by time, and yet not young,
The honeyed music of her tongue
And words of meekness scarcely told
A nature passionate and bold,   515
Strong, self-concentred, spurning guide,
Its milder features dwarfed beside
Her unbent will's majestic pride.

She sat among us, at the best
A not unfeared, half-welcome guest, 520
Rebuking with her cultured phrase
Our homeliness of words and ways.
A certain pard-like, treacherous grace
　Swayed the lithe limbs and drooped the lash,
　Lent the white teeth their dazzling flash; 525
　And under low brows, black with night,
　Rayed out at times a dangerous light;
The sharp heat-lightnings of her face
Presaging ill to him whom Fate
Condemned to share her love or hate. 530
A woman tropical, intense
In thought and act, in soul and sense,
She blended in a like degree
The vixen and the devotee,
Revealing with each freak or feint 535
　The temper of Petruchio's Kate,°
The raptures of Siena's saint.°
Her tapering hand and rounded wrist
Had facile power to form a fist;
The warm, dark languish of her eyes 540
Was never safe from wrath's surprise.
Brows saintly calm and lips devout

Knew every change of scowl and pout;
And the sweet voice had notes more high
And shrill for social battle-cry.   545
Since then what old cathedral town
Has missed her pilgrim staff and gown,
What convent-gate has held its lock
Against the challenge of her knock!
Through Smyrna's plague-hushed thoroughfares,   550
Up sea-set Malta's rocky stairs,
Grey olive slopes of hills that hem
Thy tombs and shrines, Jerusalem,
Or startling on her desert throne
The crazy Queen of Lebanon°   555
With claims fantastic as her own,
Her tireless feet have held their way;
And still, unrestful, bowed, and grey,
She watches under Eastern skies,
   With hope each day renewed and fresh,   560
   The Lord's quick coming in the flesh,
Whereof she dreams and prophesies!

Where'er her troubled path may be,
   The Lord's sweet pity with her go!
The outward wayward life we see,   565

The hidden springs we may not know.
Nor it is given us to discern
  What threads the fatal sisters spun,
  Through what ancestral years has run
The sorrow with the woman born,   570
What forged her cruel chain of moods,
What set her feet in solitudes,
  And held the love within her mute,
What mingled madness in the blood,
  A life-long discord and annoy,   575
  Water of tears with oil of joy,
And hid within the folded bud
  Perversities of flower and fruit.
It is not ours to separate
The tangled skein of will and fate,   580
To show what metes and bounds should stand
Upon the soul's debatable land,
And between choice and Providence
Divide the circle of events;
But He who knows our frame is just,   585
  Merciful, and compassionate,
And full of sweet assurances
And hope for all the language is,
  That He remembereth we are dust!

At last the great logs, crumbling low, 590
Sent out a dull and duller glow,
The bull's-eye watch that hung in view,
Ticking its weary circuit through,
Pointed with mutely-warning sign
Its black hand to the hour of nine. 595
That sign the pleasant circle broke:
My uncle ceased his pipe to smoke,
Knocked from its bowl the refuse grey,
And laid it tenderly away,
Then roused himself to safely cover 600
The dull red brands with ashes over.
And while, with care, our mother laid
The work aside, her steps she stayed
One moment, seeking to express
Her grateful sense of happiness 605
For food and shelter, warmth and health,
And love's contentment more than wealth,
With simple wishes (not the weak,
Vain prayers which no fulfilment seek,
But such as warm the generous heart, 610
O'er-prompt to do with Heaven its part)
That none might lack, that bitter night,
For bread and clothing, warmth and light.

Within our beds awhile we heard
The wind that round the gables roared,   615
With now and then a ruder shock,
Which made our very bedsteads rock.
We heard the loosened clapboards tost,
The board-nails snapping in the frost;
And on us, through the unplastered wall,   620
Felt the light sifted snow-flakes fall.
But sleep stole on, as sleep will do
When hearts are light and life is new;
Faint and more faint the murmurs grew,
Till in the summer-land of dreams   625
They softened to the sound of streams,
Low stir of leaves, and dip of oars,
And lapsing waves on quiet shores.

Next morn we wakened with the shout
Of merry voices high and clear;   630
And saw the teamsters drawing near
To break the drifted highways out.
Down the long hillside treading slow
We saw the half-buried oxen go,
Shaking the snow from heads uptost,   635
Their straining nostrils white with frost.

Before our door the straggling train
Drew up, an added team to gain.
The elders threshed their hands a-cold,
    Passed, with the cider-mug, their jokes 640
    From lip to lip; the younger folks
Down the loose snow-banks, wrestling, rolled,
Then toiled again the cavalcade
    O'er windy hill, through clogged ravine,
    And woodland paths that wound between 645
Low drooping pine-boughs winter-weighed.
From every barn a team afoot,
At every house a new recruit,
Where, drawn by Nature's subtlest law,
Haply the watchful young men saw 650
Sweet doorway pictures of the curls
And curious eyes of merry girls,
Lifting their hands in mock defence
Against the snow-ball's compliments,
And reading in each missive tost 655
The charm with Eden never lost.

We heard once more the sleigh-bells' sound;
    And, following where the teamsters led,
The wise old Doctor went his round,

Just pausing at our door to say,
In the brief autocratic way
Of one who, prompt at Duty's call,
Was free to urge her claim on all,
  That some poor neighbor sick abed
At night our mother's aid would need.
For, one in generous thought and deed,
  What mattered in the sufferer's sight
  The Quaker matron's inward light,
The Doctor's mail of Calvin's creed?
All hearts confess the saints elect
  Who, twain in faith, in love agree,
And melt not in an acid sect
  The Christian pearl of charity!

So days went on: a week had passed
Since the great world was heard from last.
The Almanac we studied o'er,
Read and reread our little store
Of books and pamphlets, scarce a score;
One harmless novel, mostly hid
From younger eyes, a book forbid,
And poetry (or good or bad,
A single book was all we had),

Where Ellwood's° meek, drab-skirted Muse,
  A stranger to the heathen Nine,
  Sang, with a somewhat nasal whine, 685
The wars of David and the Jews.
At last the floundering carrier bore
The village paper to our door.
Lo! broadening outward as we read,
To warmer zones the horizon spread; 690
In panoramic length unrolled
We saw the marvels that it told.
Before us passed the painted Creeks,°
  And daft M'Gregor on his raids
  In Costa Rica's everglades. 695
And up Taygetos winding slow
Rode Ypsilanti's Mainote Greeks,
A Turk's head at each saddle bow!
Welcome to us its week-old news,
Its corner for the rustic Muse, 700
  Its monthly gauge of snow and rain,
Its record, mingling in a breath
The wedding knell and dirge of death:
Jest, anecdote, and love-lorn tale,
The latest culprit sent to jail; 705
Its hue and cry of stolen and lost,

Its vendue sales and goods at cost,
   And traffic calling loud for gain.
We felt the stir of hall and street,
The pulse of life that round us beat;
The chill embargo of the snow
Was melted in the genial glow;
Wide swung again our ice-locked door,
And all the world was ours once more!
Clasp, Angel of the backward look
   And folded wings of ashen grey
   And voice of echoes far away,
The brazen covers of thy book;
The weird palimpsest old and vast,
Wherein thou hid'st the spectral past;
Where, closely mingling, pale and glow
The characters of joy and woe;
The monographs of outlived years,
Or smile-illumed or dim with tears,
   Green hills of life that slope to death,
And haunts of home, whose vistaed trees
Shade off to mournful cypresses
   With the white amaranths underneath.
Even while I look, I can but heed
   The restless sands' incessant fall,

Importunate hours that hours succeed,
Each clamorous with its own sharp need,
   And duty keeping pace with all.
Shut down and clasp the heavy lids;
I hear again the voice that bids 735
The dreamer leave his dream midway
For larger hopes and graver fears:
Life greatens in these later years,
The century's aloe flowers to-day!

Yet, haply, in some lull of life, 740
Some Truce of God° which breaks its strife,
The worldling's eyes shall gather dew,
   Dreaming in throngful city ways
Of winter joys his boyhood knew;
And dear and early friends — the few 745
Who yet remain — shall pause to view
   These Flemish pictures° of old days;
Sit with me by the homestead hearth,
And stretch the hands of memory forth
   To warm them at the wood-fire's blaze! 750
And thanks untraced to lips unknown
Shall greet me like the odors blown
From unseen meadows newly mown,

Or lilies floating in some pond,
Wood-fringed, the wayside gaze beyond;
The traveller owns the grateful scents
Of sweetness near, he knows not whence,
And, pausing, takes with forehead bare
The benediction of the air.

NOTES

THE ANCIENT MARINER

Motto. — I can easily believe that in the universe are more invisible beings than visible. But who shall make known to us the nature of them all, the rank, the relationships, the distinguishing features, and the offices of each? What do they do? Where do they dwell? Always about the knowledge of these wonders the mind of man has circled, never reached it. Nevertheless, I deny not, it is pleasant sometimes to contemplate in the mind, as in a picture, the image of this greater and better world; that the intellect, wonted to the petty details of daily life, be not narrowed overmuch, nor sink utterly to paltry thoughts. But, in the meantime, the truth must be vigilantly sought after, and a temperate judgment maintained, that we may distinguish things certain from things uncertain, day from night.

1. It is. "It is" is common for "there was" in the old ballads. The ballad manner is used throughout. The omission of connectives, and of such phrases as "he said," and the sudden shifts from the past tense to the present and back, you will find on almost every page of Professor Child's *English and Scottish Popular Ballads*. The metre, of alternating four and three-beat lines, four lines to the stanza, is known as ballad-metre.

Marginal note. These marginal summaries, or "glosses," with their quaintness of style, add a good deal to the effect of the yarn. It is hard to imagine what its effect would have been without them.

9–12. He holds . . . dropt he. The original reading was

> But still he holds the Wedding-Guest —
>   There was a ship, quoth he.
> "Nay, if thou's got a laughsome tale,
>   Mariner, come with me."
>
> He holds him with his skinny hand,
>   Quoth he, there was a Ship —
> "Now get thee hence, thou grey-beard Loon,
>   Or my staff shall make thee skip."

This is a little ludicrous. In the shorter final form there is nothing to provoke a smile. All of the little changes made by Coleridge after the first edition are improvements.

12. Eftsoons. At once. Throughout the poem, Coleridge uses an antique phraseology as appropriate to the time of the story.

25. Left. Sailing south.

30. Noon. On the Equator.

31. Beat his breast. The Wedding-Guest's attention is still divided, though he is fast coming under the spell of the tale.

62. Swound. Swoon.

64. Thorough. Old form of through.

69. Thunder-fit. Crash like a thunder-clap.

79. God save thee, etc. The Wedding-Guest has now forgotten all about the wedding feast he is missing. To realize how marvellously condensed the story is, and how much of its strange power depends on its condensation, you need only try to put everything that is implied on this single page of the narrative into your own prose.

83. Upon the right. That is, they have turned northward.

128. The death-fires. St. Elmo's fire. A flame-like appearance at tip of mast or yard-arm — of electrical origin. Commonly seen on dark and stormy nights.

164. They for joy did grin. Coleridge says, in his *Table-Talk*, "I took the thought of 'grinning for joy' from my companion's remark to me when we had climbed to the top of Plinlimmon, and were nearly dead with thirst. We could not speak from the constriction till we found a little puddle under a stone. He said to me, 'You grinned like an idiot.' He had done the same."

188. Is that a Death? In the first edition is a stanza describing Death. Professor Dowden surmises that he felt that "Relying largely, as he did in his poems which deal with the supernatural, on the effect produced by their psychological truth, Coleridge could afford to subdue the supernatural, and refine it to the utmost. He did not need to drag into his verse all the horrors of the churchyard and the nether pit of Hell. He felt that these hideous incidents of the grave only detracted from the finer horror of the voluptuous beauty of his White Devil, the nightmare Life-in-Death. . . . She it was, this Life-in-Death, who with her numbing spell haunted Coleridge himself in after days.'"

211. Within the nether tip. "It is a common superstition among sailors," wrote Coleridge in a manuscript note, "that

324   SELECTED POEMS

something evil is about to happen whenever a star dogs the moon."

223. My cross-bow. It has been noted that mention of the cross-bow dates the adventure of the Mariner at the sixteenth century or earlier.

290. The Albatross fell off. Like Christian's burden, in *Pilgrim's Progress*.

297. Silly. In its old meaning, "empty."

308. A blessed ghost. A spirit, blessed because freed from the prison of the body.

464. Oh! dream of joy. "How pleasantly, how reassuringly," says Walter Pater, " the whole nightmare story is made to end, among the clear fresh sounds and lights of the bay, where it began."

535. Ivy-tod. Ivy bush.

LAYS OF ANCIENT ROME

HORATIUS

" The following ballad is supposed to have been made about a hundred and twenty years after the war which it celebrates, and just before the taking of Rome by the Gauls. The author seems to have been an honest citizen, proud of the military glory of his country, sick of the disputes of factions, and much given to pining after good old times which had never really existed. The allusion, however, to the partial manner in which the public lands were allotted could proceed only from a plebeian; and the allusion to the fraudulent sale of spoils marks the date of the poem, and shows that the poet shared in the general discontent with which the proceedings of Camillus, after the taking of Veii, were regarded." — Macaulay's *Preface.*

For all proper names mentioned in the *Lays*, the student should consult a classical dictionary.

3. The great house of Tarquin. The "wrong" the Tarquins had suffered was exile from Rome for their tyranny.

72. Traced from the right. The Greeks originally wrote (as Orientals still do) from right to left.

200. The deed of shame. Tarquinius Sextus had wronged Lucretia, wife of a kinsman. This deed brought to a head the popular hatred of the Tarquins, and more than any other one thing brought about their exile from Rome.

550. The Comitium. The Forum.

THE BATTLE OF THE LAKE REGILLUS

" The following poem is supposed to have been produced about ninety years after the lay of Horatius. Some persons mentioned in the lay of Horatius make their appearance again, and some appellations and epithets used in the lay of Horatius have been purposely repeated: for, in an age of ballad-poetry, it scarcely ever fails to happen, that certain phrases come to be appropriated to certain men and things, and are regularly applied to those men and things by every minstrel. Thus we find both things in the Homeric poems and in Hesiod, βίη 'Ηρακληείη' περικλυτὸς 'Αμφιγυήεις, διάκτορος 'Αργειφόντης, ἑπτάπυλος Θήβη, 'Ἑλένης, ἕνεκ' ἠϋκόμοιο. Thus, too, in our own national songs, Douglas is almost always the doughty Douglas: England is merry England: all the gold is red; and all the ladies are gay.

"The principal distinction between the lay of Horatius and the lay of the Lake Regillus is that the former is meant to be purely Roman, while the latter, though national in its general spirit, has a slight tincture of Greek learning and Greek superstition. The battle of the Lake Regillus is in all respects a Homeric battle, except that the combatants ride astride on their horses, instead of driving chariots. The mass of fighting men is hardly mentioned. The leaders single each other out, and engage hand to hand. The great object of the warriors on both sides is, as in the *Iliad*, to obtain possession of the spoils and bodies of the slain; and several circumstances are related which forcibly remind us of the great slaughter round the corpses of Sarpedon and Patroclus.

"In the following poem, therefore, images and incidents have been borrowed, not merely without scruple, but on principle, from the incomparable battle-pieces of Homer.

"The popular belief at Rome, from an early period, seems to have been that the event of the great day of Regillus was decided by supernatural agency. Castor and Pollux, it was said, had fought, armed and mounted, at the head of the legions of the commonwealth, and had afterwards carried the news of the victory with incredible speed to the city. The well in the Forum at which they had alighted was pointed out. Near the well rose their ancient temple. A great festival was kept to their honour on the Ides of Quintilis, supposed to be the anniversary of the battle; and on that day sumptuous sacrifices were offered to them at the public charge. One spot on the margin of Lake Regillus was regarded during many ages with superstitious awe. A mark, resembling in shape a horse's hoof, was discernible in the volcanic rock; and this mark was believed to have been made by one of the celestial chargers." — Macaulay's *Preface*.

2. Lictors. Bodyguards.

13. Yellow River. The Tiber.

14. Sacred Hill. The hill on which the temple of Jupiter stood.

15. Ides of Quintilis. July the fifteenth, the day of the festival of Castor and Pollux.

63. The Thirty Cities. A great confederation of Latin cities which united in opposing Rome.

91. Did his office. Performed his duty.

174. The ghastly priest. The priest of Diana at Aricia was always a runaway slave who had killed his predecessor.

217. A woman fair and stately. The spirit of Lucretia, whom Tarquinius Sextus had wronged.

623–624. Hearth of Vesta . . . Golden Shield. The Temple of Vesta, goddess of the hearth, stood in the Forum. Here the sacred fire was kept always burning by the Vestal Virgins, and here was guarded a sacred shield, supposed to have fallen from Heaven. The Romans believed that so long as it was preserved, the city was safe. "The Twelve," mentioned below (l. 695), were the twelve priests whose duty it was to guard the Shield.

VIRGINIA

"A collection consisting exclusively of war-songs would give an imperfect, or rather an erroneous notion of the spirit of the old Latin ballads. . . . No parts of early Roman history are richer with poetical colouring than those which relate to the long contest between the privileged houses and the commonalty. The population of Rome was, from a very early period, divided into hereditary castes, which, indeed, readily united to repel foreign enemies, but which regarded each other, during many years, with bitter animosity. . . . Appius Claudius had left a name as much detested as that of Sextus Tarquinius. This elder Appius had been Consul more than seventy years before the introduction of the Licinian laws. By availing himself of a singular crisis in public feeling, he had obtained the consent of the Commons to the abolition of the Tribuneship, and had been the chief of that Council of Ten to which the whole direction of the State had been committed. In a few months his administration had become universally odious. It had been swept away by an irresistible outbreak of popular fury, and its memory was still held in abhorrence by the whole city. The immediate cause of the downfall of this execrable government was said to have been an attempt made by Appius Claudius upon the chastity of a beautiful young girl of humble birth. The story ran that the Decemvir, unable to succeed by bribes and solicitations, resorted to an outrageous act of tyranny. A vile dependant of the Claudian house laid claim to the damsel as his slave. The cause was brought before the tribunal of Appius. The wicked magistrate, in defiance of the clearest proofs, gave judgment for the claimant. But the girl's father, a brave soldier, saved her from servitude and dishonour by stabbing her to the heart in the sight of the whole Forum. That blow was the signal for a general explosion. Camp and city rose at once; the Ten were pulled down; the Tribuneship was reëstablished; and Appius escaped the hands of the executioner only by a voluntary death.

"It can hardly be doubted that a story so admirably adapted to the purposes both of the poet and of the demagogue would be eagerly seized upon by minstrels burning with hatred against the Patrician order, against the Claudian house, and especially against the grandson and namesake of the infamous Decemvir.

"In order that the reader may judge fairly of these fragments of the lay of Virginia, he must imagine himself a Plebeian who has just voted for the reëlection of Sextius and Licinius. All the power of the Patricians has been exerted to throw out the two great champions of the Commons. Every Posthumius, Æmilius, and Cornelius has used his influence to the utmost. Debtors have been let out of the workhouses on condition of voting against the men of the people: Clients have been posted to hiss and interrupt the favourite candidates: Appius Claudius Crassus has spoken with more than his usual eloquence and asperity: all has been in vain: Licinius and Sextius have a fifth time carried all the tribes: work is suspended: the booths are closed: the Plebeians bear on their shoulders the two champions of liberty through the Forum. Just at this moment it is announced that a popular poet, a zealous adherent of the Tribunes, has made a new song, which will cut the Claudian nobles to the heart. The crowd gathers round him, and calls on him to recite it. He takes his stand on the spot where, according to tradition, Virginia, more than seventy years ago, was seized by the pandar of Appius, and he begins his story." — Macaulay's *Preface*.

6. Maids with Snaky tresses. This line alludes to the stories of Medusa and Circe.

10. The wicked Ten. The Decemviri, who had been appointed to rule Rome, and had become tyrants.

20. Client. Each of the great men of Rome was surrounded by a company of dependants, or "clients," who were expected to serve him in return for his patronage.

35. Sacred Street. The Via Sacra, which led to the Forum.

46. Seven Hills. Rome was built upon seven hills.

98. Scævola. Mucius Scævola was a Roman youth condemned to be burned alive for the attempted assassination of Porsena, who was besieging Rome. He deliberately held his hand in flame, without a wince, and told Porsena there were three hundred other Roman youths as brave who had sworn to kill him. According to the legend, Scævola was freed, and peace made with Rome.

249. Caius, of Corioli. Caius Marcius, called Coriolanus, because his bravery had captured the town of Corioli. Later exiled from Rome for his indifference to the welfare of the commons. See Shakespeare's *Coriolanus*.

THE PROPHECY OF CAPYS

"It can hardly be necessary to remind any reader that according to the popular tradition, Romulus, after he had slain his grand-uncle Amulius, and restored his grandfather Numitor, determined to quit Alba, the hereditary domain of the Sylvian princes, and to found a new city. The gods, it was added, vouchsafed the clearest signs of the favour with which they regarded the enterprise, and of the high destinies reserved for the young colony.

"This event was likely to be a favourite theme of the old Latin minstrels. They would naturally attribute the project of Romulus to some divine intimation of the power and prosperity which it was decreed that his city should attain. They would probably introduce seers, foretelling the victories of unborn Consuls and Dictators; and the last great victory would generally occupy the most conspicuous place in the prediction. There is nothing strange in the supposition that the poet who was employed to celebrate the first great triumph of the Romans over the Greeks might throw his song of exultation into this form. . . .

"The following lay belongs to the latest age of Latin ballad-poetry. Nævius and Livius Andronicus were probably among the children whose mothers held them up to see the chariot of Curius go by. The minstrel who sang on that day might possibly have lived to read the first hexameters of Ennius, and to see the first comedies of Plautus. His poem, as might be expected, shows a much wider acquaintance with the geography, manners, and productions of remote nations, than would have been found in compositions of the age of Camillus. But he troubles himself little about dates, and having heard travellers talk with admiration of the Colossus of Rhodes, and of the structures and gardens with which the Macedonian kings of Syria had embellished their residence on the banks of the Orontes, he has never thought of inquiring whether these things existed in the age of Romulus."— Macaulay's *Preface*.

93. Capys. Himself of the Sylvian line, a descendant of Æneas.

150. Liber. Bacchus, god of wine.

177. Pilum. Javelin.

211. Epirotes. Dwellers in Epirus.

230. The Red King. Pyrrhus, the Grecian king who had been overcome by the Romans. The Tarentines had insulted a Roman ambassador.

"Rome, in consequence of this insult, declared war against the Tarentines. The Tarentines sought for allies beyond the Ionian Sea. Pyrrhus, king of Epirus, came to their help with a large army; and, for the first time, the two great nations of antiquity were fairly matched against each other.

"The fame of Greece in arms, as well as in arts, was then at the height. Half a century earlier, the career of Alexander had excited the admiration and terror of all nations from the Ganges to the Pillars of Hercules. Royal houses, founded by Macedonian captains, still reigned at Antioch and Alexandria. That barbarian warriors, led by barbarian chiefs, should win a pitched battle against Greek valour, guided by Greek science, seemed as incredible as it would now seem that the Burmese or the Siamese should, in the open plain, put to flight an equal number of the best English troops. The Tarentines were convinced that their countrymen were irresistible in war; and this conviction had emboldened them to treat with the grossest indignity one whom they regarded as the representative of an inferior race. Of the Greek generals then living, Pyrrhus was indisputably the first. Among the troops who were trained in the Greek discipline, his Epirotes ranked high. His expedition to Italy was a turning-point in the history of the world. He found there a people who, far inferior to the Athenians and Corinthians in the fine arts, in the speculative sciences, and in all the refinements of life, were the best soldiers on the face of the earth.

"The conquerors had a good right to exult in their success; for the glory was all their own. They had not learned from their enemy how to conquer him. It was with their own national arms, and in their own national battle-array, that they had overcome weapons and tactics long believed to be invincible. The pilum and the broadsword had vanquished the Macedonian spear. The legion had broken the Macedonian phalanx. Even the elephants, when the surprise produced by their first appearance was over, could cause no disorder in the steady yet flexible battalions of Rome." — Macaulay's *Preface*.

266. Suppliant's Grove. A hollow at the crest of the Capitoline Hill, where, as in the Temple of Vesta, an asylum or place of refuge could be found by criminals or those who were in fear of violence.

THE RAVEN

Some time after *The Raven* had been written and gained a wide hearing, Poe wrote an essay called *The Philosophy of Composition*. "*The Raven*," says Arthur Ransome, one of Poe's best critics, "a profound piece of technique, is scarcely as profound, and certainly not as surprising, as *The Philosophy of Composition*, in which its construction is minutely analyzed; and Poe callously explains, as a matter of scientific rather than personal interest, that the whole poem was built on the refrain, Nevermore, and that this particular refrain was chosen on account of the sonority and ease of the *o* and *r* sounded together."

Poe was fond of exaggerating for the sake of making a point, and in *The Philosophy of Composition* was arguing that the act of composing poetry follows regular laws. At all events, there is no doubt that the long sound "ore" had a fascination for him. The words "no more" are prominent in half a dozen of his short poems; and Lenore is the title of one of them.

The subject of the poem is Poe's favorite one. See *Introduction*, p. xxi.

16–17. Chamber Door. These repetitions, or repetends, of phrases or whole lines, are a most striking trait of Poe's verse. It is fair to guess that he got the idea from Coleridge's *Ancient Mariner*. See p. 7, lines 115, 117, 119.

38. Raven. The raven was always considered a bird of evil omen.

41. Pallas. Pallas Athene, or Minerva, was the goddess of conflict as well as the goddess of wisdom.

64. Burden. Refrain.

89. Balm in Gilead. *Jeremiah* viii. 22.

93. Aidenn. The Arabic form of "Eden."

THE VISION OF SIR LAUNFAL

The Holy Grail plays an important part in the legends of the Middle Ages. The Grail was the fabled cup from which Christ had drunk at the Last Supper. It was supposed to have been brought to England by Joseph of Arimathea. Tennyson represents the Knights of the Round Table setting out in search of the Grail. Most of them " pursue wandering fires " — do not find the Grail, and in the meantime neglect their natural duties at home.

So the young knight Sir Launfal is inspired to a quest of the Grail, which he fancies to be a virtuous enterprise, but which is really a selfish pursuit of his own glory. See *Introduction*, p. xxiv.

Prelude to Part First

The opening lines suggest that the poet begins " improvising," and gradually finds his way, chord by chord, to a prelude, — composed in the key, and suggesting the theme, of the movement which is to follow. Summer and youth and hope are the subject of this Prelude, and the young and brilliant Sir Launfal appears naturally upon the scene at the end : and so the tale begins.

9. Not only around our infancy, etc. The allusion is to the famous passage in Wordsworth's *Intimations of Immortality*: Lowell says the vision is still there, if we only had eyes to see it.

> "Heaven lies about us in our infancy !
>   Shades of the prison-house begin to close
>   Upon the growing boy.
>   But he beholds the light, and whence it flows,
>   He sees it in his joy;

SELECTED POEMS

> The youth, who daily farther from the east
> Must travel, still is Nature's priest,
>   And by the vision splendid
>   Is on his way attended;
> At length the man perceives it die away
> And fade into the light of common day."

12. We Sinais climb. We come face to face with God, as Moses did on Mount Sinai.

116. In the North Countree. The action is supposed to take place in the North of England; but the setting, the scenery as Lowell paints it, belongs to New England.

Prelude to Part Second

As the first prelude gave the keynote of summer and youth and joy, the second strikes a sombre chord of age and winter. Winter is the fit season for the aged and broken knight to appear again.

243. The Weaver Winter. The first edition read, "For the frost's swift shuttles its shroud had spun." Which is better?

276. The leper, etc. The same test is applied to the aged knight, but he has learned the meaning of life. Like the *Ancient Mariner*, he has discovered that love of one's fellow-creatures is the key to real success.

291. Leprosie. The form, like "Countree," is used to give a touch of quaintness to the style.

320–327. These lines give the "moral" of the whole poem.

SOHRAB AND RUSTUM

For the sources of the poem, see *Introduction*, p. xxvii. The poem is called "an episode," in the subtitle. That is, it is supposed to be a fragment of a larger epic. This is suggested by the " and " with which the tale begins.

2. Oxus. This great river bounded Persia, and formed a natural bar between the Persians and the Tartar hordes of Central Asia.

11; Peran-Wisa. The chief in command of the Tartar Army for Afrasiab, king of the Tartars.

62. Fame speaks clear. The young Sohrab, like the heroes of the *Iliad*, looks upon war as a game at which a higher personal stake is to be won than at any other game.

110–116. From their black tents. These lines have the stately stride of Arnold's master, in English, of the noble or "grand" style, — Milton.

230. That one slight helpless girl. You remember Sohrab's mother had deceived Rustum as to the sex of their child.

257. Unknown and in plain arms. As Sir Lancelot fought for similar reasons. See Tennyson's *Lancelot and Elaine*.

302. As some rich woman, etc. The long simile that follows is in the Homeric manner — not only a figure of comparison, but a complete little picture in itself. Arnold said of the figures in this poem, " I can only say that I took a great deal of trouble to orientalize them, because I thought they looked strange, and jarred, if western." As we have seen, Lowell took no such pains with *The Vision of Sir Launfal* in which the scenery and figures are modern, while the subject of the tale is mediæval. But *The Vision* was a rapid sketch, while *Sohrab and Rustum* is a work of art composed with extreme care.

322. O thou young man, etc. Here again Arnold follows Homer as a model. The old Greek champions, like the warriors

338 SELECTED POEMS

of all primitive races, prefaced their combats with boasts and warnings.

828. Thou dreadful man. Dreadful is one of the many words, used rightly in this poem, which we commonly degrade.

875. But the majestic river floated on. The Oxus throughout stands as a great and calm witness of the human tragedy recorded in the poem — a symbol of the permanence of nature and life, whatever may befall the human race.

THE COURTSHIP OF MILES STANDISH

Miles Standish was, of course, a real historic figure. Of good English blood, and next in succession to large estates in England, he chose to throw in his fortunes with the Puritan settlers at Plymouth. He came of fighting stock, and was held in awe by the Indians.

15. John Alden, according to the chronicle, "was hired for a cooper at Southampton, where the ship the *Mayflower* victualled; and being a hopeful young man was much desired, but left to his own liking to go or stay when he came here to Plymouth, but he stayed and married here." Longfellow traced his descent to both Standish and Alden.

28. Arcabucero. Musketeer.

85. "Mr. William Mullines and his wife and two children, Joseph and Priscilla," are in the list of passengers in the *Mayflower*. They all died except Priscilla during that first terrible winter of which Rose Standish was another victim.

442. The elder of Plymouth. Elder William Brewster, who had been chosen as their minister before the *Mayflower* sailed from the old world.

449-481. Winslow's *Relation* gives the story as follows: —

"At length came one of them to us, who was sent by Conanacus, their chief sachem or king, accompanied with one Tokamahamon, a friendly Indian. This messenger inquired for Tisquantum, our interpreter, who not being at home, seemed rather to be glad than sorry, and leaving for him a bundle of new arrows, lapped in a rattlesnake's skin, desired to depart with all expedition." . . . Hereupon, after some deliberation, the Governor stuffed the skin with powder and shot, and sent it back, returning no less defiance to Conanacus."

751. Two, from among them advancing. Longfellow has shifted the scene of the incident that follows, but otherwise follows Winslow's *Relation* pretty closely.

"Divers of them severally, or few together, came to the plantation to him (Captain Standish), where they would whet and sharpen the points of their knives before his face, and use many other insulting gestures and speeches. Among the rest Wituwamat bragged of the excellency of his knife. On the end of the handle there was pictured a woman's face; 'But,' said he, 'I have another at home, wherewith I have killed both French and English, and that hath a man's face on it; and by and by these two must marry.' Further he said of that knife he there had, 'Hinnaim namen, hinnaim michen, matta cuts'; that is to say, 'By and by it should see, and by and by it should eat, but not speak.' Also Pecksuot, being a man of greater stature than the Captain, told him, though he were a great captain, yet he was but a little man; 'And,' said he, 'though I be no sachem, yet I am a man of great strength and courage.' These things the Captain observed, yet bare with patience for the present.

"On the next day, seeing he could not get many of them together at once, and this Pecksuot and Wituwamat both together, with another man, and a youth of some eighteen years of age, which was brother to Wituwamat and, villain-like, trod in his steps, daily putting many tricks upon the weaker sort of men, and having about as many of his own company in a room with them, gave the word to his men, and the door being fast shut, began with Pecksuot, and snatching his own knife from his neck, though with much struggling, killed him therewith, the point whereof he had made as sharp as a needle, and ground the back also to an edge. Wituwamat and the other man the rest killed, and took the youth, whom the Captain caused to be hanged. But it is incredible how many wounds these two pineses [braves] received before they died, not making any fearful noise, but catching at their weapons and striving to the last. Hobbamock stood by all this time as a spectator, and meddled not, observing how our men demeaned themselves in this action. All being here ended, smiling he brake forth into these speeches to the captain: 'Yesterday Pecksuot, bragging of his own strength and stature, said, though you were a great captain, yet you were but a little man; but to-day I see you are big enough to lay him on the ground.'"

1006. Happy husband and wife. There is a quaint entry written many years later in Bradford's account: "Mr. William Mollines and his wife, his son and his servant, died the first winter. Only his daughter Priscilla survived and married with John Alden, who are both living and have eleven children."

SNOW-BOUND

65. Pisa's leaning miracle. The leaning tower of Pisa.

90. Amun. An Egyptian god with a ram's head.

215. The Chief of Gambia, etc. This and the italicized lines below are from a poem called *The African Chief* in a school-book of Whittier's, *The American Preceptor*.

259. Cocheco. Now Dover, N.H.

286. Painful Sewel's ancient tome. William Sewel's *History of the Quakers*, a book which had a natural place in the Whittiers' scant library.

289. Chalkley's Journal. Chalkley was a Quaker preacher whose life was not without its adventures.

305. The tangled ram. *Genesis* xxii.

320. Apollonius ... Hermes. Apollonæus Tynæus and Hermes Trismegistus, the first a Greek and the second an Egyptian, both magicians.

332. White of Selborne. Gilbert White, author of one of the most famous books of natural history, *The Natural History of Selborne*. He lived in the eighteenth century.

398. Now bathed within the fadeless green. Whittier was never married, but a deep affection lay between him and his sister Elizabeth, who had but just died when *Snow-Bound* was written.

476. Araxes. Or Aracthus. A river whose source is in the Pindus range in Greece.

510. Another guest. This guest, who so interested Whittier, must have formed an odd contrast to the staid Quaker hosts. She was Miss Harriet Livermore. She became a religious fanatic.

536. Petruchio's Kate. Heroine of *The Taming of the Shrew*.

537. Siena's saint. St. Catherine.

555. The crazy Queen of Lebanon. Lady Hester Stanhope, like Miss Livermore, believed that Christ was very soon coming back on earth. She built a palace on Mount Lebanon, and lived there in the expectation of welcoming the Messiah on his return. Miss Livermore and she were friends for a time, but quarrelled as to which should have first place by the Redeemer.

683. Ellwood. Thomas Ellwood, a Quaker poet and friend of Milton.

693–698. Whittier even recalls the news of his boyhood, — the removal of the Creek Indians from Georgia to the west, the filibustering of one McGregor (1822) in Central America, and the struggle of the Greeks against Turkey.

741. Truce of God. "A name given to an historic compact in force during the eleventh, twelfth, and thirteenth centuries, generally applying throughout Western Europe, whereby the barons were to do no fighting from Wednesday evening till Monday morning, or during Advent or Lent, or on principal saints' days. Pilgrims, priests, women, and merchants were to receive special exemption from pillage. Violation of the truce was punishable by excommunication from the Church."

747. Flemish pictures. The Flemish painters were particularly fond of farm scenes.

THE following pages contain advertisements of Macmillan publications on kindred subjects

A PARTIAL LIST OF THE
GOLDEN TREASURY SERIES

Edited by F. T. PALGRAVE

Cloth   16mo   Each, $1.00 net

Addison, Joseph. Essays.
Arnold, Matthew. Poems.
Autocrat of the Breakfast Table.
Bacon, Sir Francis. Essays.
Ballad Book.
Book of Golden Deeds.
Book of Worthies.
Byron, Lord. Poems.
Campbell, Thomas. Poems.
Children's Garland.
Children's Treasury of Lyrical Poems.
Epictetus, Golden Sayings of.
Golden Treasury Psalter.
House of Atreus. By Æschylus.
Jest Book. By Mark Lemon.
Keats, John. Poems.
Landor, W. S. Poems.
London Lyrics.
Lyric Love.
Marcus Aurelius Antoninus, Thoughts of.
Miscellanies. By E. Fitzgerald.
Moore, Thomas. Poems.
Pilgrim's Progress. By John Bunyan.
Religio Medici. By Sir T. Browne.
Robinson Crusoe. By D. Defoe.
Rossetti, C. Poems.
Rubaiyat of Omar Khayyam.
Shakespeare, W. Songs and Sonnets.
Shelley, P. B. Poems.
Southey, R. Poems.
Tales from Shakespeare. By C. Lamb.
Tennyson, Lord Alfred.
  Idylls of the King.
  In Memoriam.
  Lyrical Poems.
  The Princess.
Theologica Germanica.
Tom Brown's School Days. By T. Hughes.
Trial and Death of Socrates.
Wordsworth. Poems.

The Golden Treasury of the Best Songs and Lyrical Poems in the English Language. Two volumes in one, $1.50.

A Complete Catalogue of this Series sent on Request

The Macmillan Company, Publishers, New York

English Poetry

Its Principles and Progress with Representative Masterpieces and Notes. By CHARLES MILLS GAYLEY, Litt.D., LLD., Professor of the English Language and Literature in the University of California, and CLEMENT C. YOUNG, of the Lowell High School, San Francisco, California.

Cloth, 12mo, $1.50 net

A manual for the general reader who takes an interest in the materials and history of the higher English poetry, and seeks a simple statement of its principles in relation to life, conduct, and art. The introduction on "The Principles of Poetry" aims to answer the questions that inevitably arise when poetry is the subject of discussion, and to give the questioner a grasp upon the essentials necessary to appreciation and to the formation of an independent judgment.

"The Introduction on 'The Principles of Poetry' should be an inspiration to both teacher and pupil, and a very definite help in appreciation and study, especially in the portion that deals with the 'Rhythm of Verse.' The remarks on the different centuries, in their literary significance and development, are helpful, and the notes to each poem, lucid and sufficient."—HARRY S. ROSS, Worcester Academy, Worcester, Mass.

For more advanced students

A History of English Prosody

From the Twelfth Century to the Present Day. In three volumes. By GEORGE SAINTSBURY, M.A. (Oxon.), Hon. LL.D. (Aberdeen), Professor of Rhetoric and English Literature in the University of Edinburgh. Volume I — From the Origins to Spenser.

Cloth, 8vo, xvii + 428 pages, $1.50 net

"What strikes one is the sensibleness of the book as a whole. Not merely for enthusiasts on metrics, but for students of literature in general, it is a good augury toward the probable clearing up of this entire blurred and cloudy subject to find Omond's mild fairness and Thomson's telling simplicity followed so soon by this all-pervading common sense. . . . The most extraordinary thing about this volume is that, unintentionally as it would appear, the author has produced the one English book now existing which is likely to be of real use to those who wish to perfect themselves in the formal side of verse composition." — *The Evening Post, New York.*

THE MACMILLAN COMPANY
Publishers   64–66 Fifth Avenue   New York

A History of English Poetry

By W. J. COURTHOPE, C.B., D.Litt., LL.D., Late Professor of Poetry in the University of Oxford.

Cloth, 8vo, $3.25 net per volume

VOLUME I. The Middle Ages — Influence of the Roman Empire — The Encyclopædic Education of the Church — The Federal System.

VOLUME II. The Renaissance and the Reformation — Influence of the Court and the Universities.

VOLUME III. English Poetry in the Seventeenth Century — Decadent Influence of the Feudal Monarchy — Growth of the National Genius.

VOLUME IV. Development and Decline of the Poetic Drama — Influence of the Court and the People.

VOLUME V. The Constitutional Compromise of the Eighteenth Century — Effects of the Classical Renaissance — Its Zenith and Decline — The Early Romantic Renaissance.

VOLUME VI. The Romantic Movement in English Poetry.

"It is his privilege to have made a contribution of great value and signal importance to the history of English literature." — *Pall Mall Gazette.*

THE MACMILLAN COMPANY
Publishers   64-66 Fifth Avenue   **New York**

The Rhetoric of Oratory
By EDWIN DU BOIS SHURTER

Cloth 12mo $1.10 net

"An unusually sensible and scientific treatment of the subject, as helpful to the graduate who is already in the game of life as to teacher and student in secondary school and college. It deals with the rhetoric of oratory, rather than the elocution of oratory." — *Journal of Education.*

Select Orations Illustrating American Political History
By SAMUEL B. HARDING

Cloth 12mo $1.25 net

Every oration in this volume has exerted some great influence on political action or political opinion, and reveals better than anything else the real spirit of the country at the time when it was delivered. The essays were selected by Samuel B. Harding, Professor of History in Indiana University, while John M. Clapp, Professor of English in Lake Forest University, supplied the introduction on oratorical style and structure.

Argumentation and Debate
By CRAVEN LAYCOCK and ROBERT L. SCALES

Cloth 12mo $1.10 net

In this work the peculiar difficulties which stand in the way of making a text-book at once teachable, practical, and easily understood, for use in teaching argumentation and debate, have been overcome. The treatment of the topics presented — the proposition, the issues, preliminary reading, evidence, kinds of arguments, fallacies, brief-drawing, the principles of presentation, refutation, and debate — is lucid and interesting as well as highly profitable.

The Macmillan Company, Publishers, New York